The Concept of Cultural Systems

A Key to Understanding Tribes and Nations

The Concept
of
Cultural Systems

A Key to Understanding Tribes and Nations

Leslie A. White

Columbia University Press
New York

Library of Congress Cataloging in Publication Data

White, Leslie A   1900–1975.
  The concept of cultural systems.

  Bibliography: p.
  1. Culture.   2. Ethnology.   I. Title.
GN357.W47   301.2   75-33003
ISBN 0-231-03961-1

Copyright © 1975 by Columbia University Press
Printed in the United States of America

To R. L. Wilder,
Mathematician, Culturologist, Friend

EDITORIAL NOTE

LESLIE A. WHITE died on March 31, 1975. The manuscript for this essay was already in the hands of Columbia University Press at that time. As one of Dr. White's literary executors, I undertook editorial responsibility for this monograph. The editing that has been done has consisted mainly of providing additional bibliographic entries. The text remains essentially as submitted.

Dr. White's influence on the field of anthropology is just now beginning to be realized, not only in ethnology but in archeology and physical anthropology as well. Perhaps his major impact has been in defining, delineating, and applying the concept of culture to a science of culturology. This essay represents White's most mature thinking on the nature of, and the science of, culture.

BETH DILLINGHAM
University of Cincinnati
September 1975

CONTENTS

PREFACE

FOR A number of years I found myself coming more and more to use the concept of cultural systems, in my thinking and occasionally in my writing, as a corollary of the proposition that "culture constitutes a distinct order of phenomena" and in recognition of the systemic character of cultural phenomena in actuality. If, then, culture is to be dealt with as systems, one must understand the structure and behavior of such systems. This understanding requires a consideration of systems in general: physical, astronomic, atomic, molecular, cellular, multicellular, social, etc. This consideration brings to the fore the injunction that *systems must be interpreted and understood in terms of themselves, i.e., their structure and behavior.* The application of this rule to cultural systems made me realize that "the function of culture is to serve the needs of man" is as invalid as it had been "obvious" to me before. "Culture is a thing, or process, *sui generis*" means just what it says; and "culture is to be explained in terms of culture" still holds.

I was thus led, by the acceptance of certain propositions that had become well established in ethnology, and by the concept of *systems,* well established in the philosophy of science, to see culture in a new light. No longer was it viewed as a handmaiden of Homo sapiens, to preserve and comfort him, but as a sector of reality in its own right whose behavior was governed by laws of its own. The analogy with language is inevitable. Language(s) could not exist without man. But language, as a distinct order of phenomena—with its structure and processes of lexicon, grammar, syntax, phonetics, phonemics—is not to be explained in terms of man as a human animal; man is not an explanatory device in the science of linguistics. So it is with culture. It too could not exist without the existence of the human species. But a consideration of man as a biological entity is irrelevant to an explanation of why tribe A reckons descent patrilineally whereas tribe B has matrilineal descent; or why one nation has a monarchical form of government whereas another has a system of parliamentary government.

The science of culture, like other sciences, is the product of an evolutionary development. Everything in the essay that follows existed in more or less explicit form in the intellectual tradition of the Western world (and possibly in the Orient and India, for aught I know) for well over a century. This intellectual tradition in general and the science of culture in particular can be explained in terms of cultural innovation, growth, and synthesis. We observe the groping toward a conception of cultural systems in the nineteenth century in the lives and works of Herbert Spencer, E. B. Tylor, and Émile Durkheim. It is rather astonishing to discover how clear and explicit it had become in the writing of Sidney Webb (1889). The picture of the twentieth century is one of confusion and contradiction, with the influence of Boas opposing the conception of cultural systems, but with progress toward a science of culture made by his students Robert H. Lowie and A. L. Kroeber, and the trend toward "cultures as wholes" initiated by Ruth Benedict (also a student of Boas). The Functionalists, with roots both in France and in England, made further progress.

What I have tried to do in the following essay is to make the trends of the past more explicit, to organize the various conceptions dealing with culture into a coherent theory and, finally, to apply this interpretation to modern cultures as well as those on the preliterate level of development. In the latter, the concept of cultural systems has done much to solve the problem of the origin of incest taboos, to make clear the function and operation of the rules of exogamy and endogamy, the origin of clan organization, etc. In the area of modern culture it has illuminated the nature of the State in general and the role of the head of the state in particular. It has clarified the nature of "justice" in a "democratic" society. It has laid bare the principles upon which the behavior of a nation rests, and has revealed the limitations of its capacity for "intelligent" behavior. Finally, it has raised the question of the survival of the saurian state.

Professor R. L. Wilder, with whom I have had many profitable discussions about cultural systems, persuaded me to take time out from *Modern Capitalist Culture*—a book I have been working on for several years—to write this essay on cultural systems. I dedicate it to him with affection in appreciation of our comradeship.

Karin Jaehne has rendered invaluable assistance in many ways in the preparation of the manuscript for which I am very grateful.

LESLIE A. WHITE
University of California
Santa Barbara

PROLOGUE

SCIENTIFIC theory turned its attention to human affairs after a few thousand years of preoccupation with the physical world and with biological organisms. During recent centuries it has been groping toward a concept of culture and a new science: culturology (see "On the Expansion of the Scope of Science," White 1947). Many scholars have sensed this trend and have given expression to it. Gustav Klemm published *Allgemeine Culturwissenschaft* in 1854–55. Edward Burnett Tylor entitled chapter 1 of *Primitive Culture* (1871) "The Science of Culture." His contemporary, Herbert Spencer, anticipated the concept of cultural systems in "A Society is an Organism," chapter 2 of *The Principles of Sociology* (1876–96). Émile Durkheim contributed an excellent exposition of the culturological point of view in *Les Règles de la méthode sociologique* (1895); however, it was so disguised by psychological terminology that its significance was unrecognized—and consequently misunderstood—not only by scholars abroad, but also by some of his colleagues. A German chemist-turned-philosopher, Wilhelm Ostwald, defined the science of culture and gave it its proper name—culturology—in *Energetische Grundlagen der Kulturwissenschaft* (1909) and more especially in "The System of the Sciences" (1916).

In the United States, A. L. Kroeber came close to a science of culture in "The Superorganic" (1917) and other essays. The conception of such a science was made explicit by R. H. Lowie in *Culture and Ethnology* (1917) and in "Cultural Anthropology: A Science" (1936), by George P. Murdock in "The Science of Culture" (1932), and by other scholars.

It has been difficult for many scholars, and impossible for some, to grasp the conception and the vision of culturology; some have launched harsh criticism of those who are trying to develop this science (see Introduction to the 1969 edition of White, *The Science of Culture*).

For the benefit of readers who may not be familiar with the history of ethnology—and especially the history of the emergence and development of culturology—frequent references to pertinent literature have been provided.

It is hoped that this essay will make clear to the reader the extent to which we are indebted to our predecessors. Many were groping, many sensed the unique nature of cultural phenomena and gave more or less explicit expression to many of the basic assumptions of culturology and the interpretations it has to offer. *The Concept of Cultural Systems* is an attempt to make the thought of our predecessors more explicit and to present it as a coherent treatise.

the concept of culture

THE basic concepts of culturology are the concept of culture and the concept of cultural systems. I have dealt with the former in an earlier essay (White 1959a) and shall refer to it from time to time in the present one.

Systemic organization is encountered everywhere. By *system* we mean an aggregation of things and events joined in interaction and interdependence to form an integral whole. In the physical realm systemic organization is manifested in atoms, molecules, stars, galaxies—the universe itself may be a system for aught we know. In the biological realm cells and multicellular organisms are systems. Associations of living beings (societies) constitute systems. And, finally, there are cultural systems. But when we say that systemic organization is to be found wherever we look, we are not saying that everything is systemically organized; disorder and chaos are still valid concepts.

Before I discuss cultural systems as such, I must say something about the fact that diverse conceptions of culture are still current (White 1954, p. 462). Man is a unique animal: only man has the ability to originate, determine, and bestow meaning upon things and events in the external world. He does this by virtue of an ability that I have called the ability to symbol (White 1962; White 1969, p. xxxviii). This class of things and events—dependent upon symboling—is the most important and fundamental category in the sciences of man. But due to the immaturity of these sciences, there is no name in the lexicon of science for these things and events. I have ventured to give them a name: *symbolates* (White 1959a, pp. 230–31).

When symbolates are considered in terms of their relationship to the human organism we call them, collectively, *behavior,* the scientific study of which is *psychology.* When we treat symbolates, not in terms of their relationship to the human organism but in terms of their relationship to one another, we call them, collectively, *culture,** the scientific study of which is *culturology.* The distinction made here is the same made in the scientific treatment of words. When we are concerned with the relationship of words to the human organism we have *speech;* the scientific study of which may involve anatomy, physiology, and psychology. When, however, we are concerned with the relationship of words to one another we have *language,* the scientific study of which is linguistics—lexicon, syntax, grammar, phonetics, etc. (White 1959a, pp. 230–33).

To reduce the above characterization of culture to a simpler and less sophisticated level, we say that culture consists of language, customs, institutions, codes, tools,

* We "call" or designate a class of phenomena "culture"; we do not say that the phenomena *are* culture. It is a bit distressing to note that reputable scholars talk as if there were an identity between a thing and the designation of the thing, or that the meaning of a noun is inherent in it, or derived from the thing that it designates. Thus, we find Kroeber and Kluckhohn (1952, p. 155) telling us what "culture basically *is*"; Honigmann (1964, p. 156) saying that "culture basically is behavior"; Hall (1968, p. 89), that it "is basically a communicative process." Cohen (1968, p. 13) takes "exception to Kroeber's assertion that nonhuman living forms do not have culture." Cohen does not say that Kroeber wishes to use the word "culture" in one way while he prefers another.

Culture is not basically anything. Culture is a word-concept. It is manmade and may be used arbitrarily to designate anything; we may define the concept as we please. To say that culture "basically is" this or that is reminiscent of the secularized version of the biblical account of how Adam named the animals: "he called a creature a horse because it *was* a horse"—basically, no doubt.

techniques, concepts, beliefs, etc.—E. B. Tylor's "classic" definition (Tylor 1871, p. 1.).

If the concept and definition of culture were as universally accepted as is the concept of copper, carbon, or iron, then one could properly say that this *is* culture— rather than behavior. But social scientists are far from consensus on this point. In fact, Kroeber and Kluckhohn (1952) have collected scores of definitions of culture—or ⋅ at least, ways of saying what culture "is." Therefore, it is unjustifiable to say that such and such *is* culture; we can only say "this is the way I use the word." In my files I have only one instance of this practice, however: Huxley (1955, p. 10) says: *"Culture* is the *appellation* [emphasis added] by which anthropologists denote this central subject of their science." As A. N. Whitehead (1911, pp. 87–88) noted many years ago: "Now it cannot be too clearly understood that, in science, technical terms are names arbitrarily assigned, like Christian names to children. There can be no question of the names being right or wrong."

Culture, as we use the term, is thus a distinct and a logically independent order of phenomena. In actuality, of course, there is no culture apart from Homo sapiens. But as an object of scientific study and interpretation, culture may be considered without reference to the human species. If this seems unrealistic to some scholars—as it does—we may remind them that the English language could have no existence apart from the human species, but we must consider it apart from its human carriers when we study its structure and processes. The same can be said of mathematical or physical concepts, the evolution of currency, the evolution of the steam engine, clan organization, or corporate structure, etc.

The autonomy of culture, its logical independence of its human carriers, has been sensed by scholars for many years: culture constitutes a process *sui generis*. "Culture, while it exists only through or in men, has an existence of its own" (Kroeber 1928, p. 493). "The reality of a social tradition as a separate aspect of the universe is no longer doubted" (Lowie 1937, p. 256). Many years earlier, the ever-astonishing Durkheim observed that "collective ways of acting or thinking [i.e., culture] have a reality outside . . . individuals . . . they exist in their own right" (Durkheim 1938 [1895], p. lvi). He later speaks of "a whole world of sentiments, ideas and images which, once born, obey laws all their own. They attract each other, repel each other, unite, divide themselves, and multiply. . . . The life thus brought into being even enjoys so great an independence that it *sometimes indulges in manifestations with no purpose or utility of any sort, for the mere pleasure of affirming itself*" (Durkheim 1947 [1912], p. 424; emphasis added). And, says Redfield (1941, p. 134), "culture . . . seems to grow by itself."

Culture, the culture process, is an interactive process; it is composed of culture traits that interact with one another, forming new permutations, combinations, and syntheses. "They [social facts, culture traits] attract each other, repel each other, unite, divide themselves, and multiply," (Durkheim 1947 [1912], p. 424; see also Durkheim 1938, p. li).

Culture traits act and react among themselves in accordance with the principle of cause and effect. Thus, culture determines and causes culture; culture is to be explained in terms of culture. "The determining cause of a social fact [culture trait] should be sought among the social facts preceding it" (Durkheim 1938, p. 110). "Culture is a thing *sui generis* which can be explained only in terms of itself" (Lowie 1917a, p. 66). "The immediate causes of cultural phenomena," according to Kroeber, "are other cultural phenomena" (1939, p. 1).

The proposition that culture is to be explained in terms of culture has evoked protest, and even resentment, in some quarters. Some psychologists have interpreted it as a denial of the relevance of psychology in the realm of "man and culture" (see the "vehement" objection by Weston LaBarre in *The Human Animal,* p. 351); they regard the culturologist as being "against psychology." But this is due to a lack of understanding on their part. They fail to see that symbolates may be interpreted meaningfully in both psychological and culturological contexts. Their reasoning (or reflex) is that if one is interested in culturology he must be against psychology, that if one is concerned with the grammar of a language he must be opposed to an interest in the conceptual and emotional factors involved in speech. There is, and can be, no justifiable conflict between psychology and culturology; on the contrary, both are necessary for a comprehensive understanding of any human event (i.e., symbolate). The psychologist, qua psychologist, cannot explain the origin of the constellation of culture traits known as the mother-in-law taboo; this explanation is the province of the culturologist. But it is the province of the psychologist to determine and make intelligible to us the behavior—the emotions, attitudes, and acts—of the man, his wife, and her mother in this little domestic drama (see White 1959a, pp. 232–34; White 1969, pp. xxx–xxxiii).

If cultural phenomena are to be explained in terms of cultural phenomena, what is to be said about the relationship between human beings as a class (biological) of phenomena, and cultural things and events as a suprabiological, extrasomatic class of phenomena?

It is man who has made the existence of culture possible. Culture, in general, is what it is because man is the kind of animal that he is; had he been different, culture would have been correspondingly different (see White,

1959b, p. 11). No one would argue that the Chinese speak the language that they do, or eat with chopsticks, because of biological structure or genetic constitution. The same principle holds for tribalism, representative government, codes of ethics, spiritual values, and rickshaws. We may, and must, assume that man's biological makeup makes a wide variety of cultures possible but imposes certain limits upon the content and scope of culture, even though we do not know the extent of these limitations. We thus arrive at two fundamental propositions: (1) man is necessary for the existence of culture, but (2) man is not necessary for a scientific explanation of variations of culture.

The behavior of all living species, with the exception of Homo sapiens, is determined by its biological makeup: its genetic constitution, bodily structure, etc. The behavior of Homo sapiens includes both behavior dependent upon symboling and behavior independent of symboling. The former we call human behavior (by definition); it is unique in the animal world. The latter is merely mammalian, primate, behavior (coughing, stretching, yawning, etc.). Man's nonhuman behavior, like that of other animals, is determined by his biological makeup. His human behavior, however, is not biologically determined; it is determined by the culture in which the human animal lives: *The human behavior of peoples is determined by their respective cultures.* (I say *peoples* because the human behavior of individuals is affected, but not determined, by their biological makeup.) If one is born and reared in Tibetan culture he becomes a Tibetan; in Eskimo culture he becomes an Eskimo.

> *man does not and cannot control his culture*
> *or direct its course*

If the culture process is a process *sui generis,* and if cultural phenomena are determined by cultural phenomena, it follows that man lies outside the cause-and-effect sequence of cultural events. As a biological datum, man lies outside the cultural process; he enters it as a human being, but as a human being he is a constellation of cultural elements, a capsule of culture. The belief that man can control his culture, like other illusions, is made possible and nourished by a profound and comprehensive ignorance of the nature, structure, and behavior of cultural systems. The situation is like that of rain dances: the belief that man could bring rain by dancing was possible only because of ignorance of meteorological phenomena. The hardy perennials of illusion flourish in the fertile soil of ignorance (see "Man's Control over Civilization: an Anthropocentric Illusion" in White, *The Science of Culture*).

what is "the function of culture"?

At this point I must reverse a position that I have held for years. In *The Evolution of Culture* (1959b) I wrote: "The purpose and function of culture are to make life secure and enduring for the human species" (p. 8). This was repeated in "The Concept of Culture" (White with Dillingham 1973): "The answer to the question, What is the function of culture? is very simple and obvious . . . it is to make life secure and enduring for the human species" (p. 12). It was the concept of cultural systems that made it possible for me to see the error of this "simple and obvious" explanation. It was simple and obvious to the pre-Copernican that the earth was motionless and that the sun rose and set.

The notion that it is the function of culture to serve man's needs, to make life secure and enduring for him, is not only anthropocentric, it also smacks of the theological:

> And God said, Behold, I have given you every herb yielding seed . . . and every tree, in which is the fruit of

> a tree yielding seed; to you it shall be for food. . . . Be
> fruitful and multiply, and replenish the earth, and sub-
> due it; and have dominion over the fish of the sea, and
> over the birds of the heavens, and over every living thing
> that moveth upon the earth (Gen. 1).

What geologist or astronomer would say that it is the
function of the earth to minister to man's needs and make
his occupancy of the planet secure and enduring? *Webster's New International Dictionary,* 3d ed., defines function as "the action for which a person or thing is specially
fitted, used, or responsible or for which a thing exists." To
be sure, the earth supports life; man avails himself of the
planet's resources, and the energy of the life-giving sun.
But to say that it is the *function* of the solar system to
nourish and protect this puny primate is to get back to
Genesis. If the earth makes life possible—and even satisfying and pleasurable at times—it also devastates whole
regions and exterminates life on a grand scale with
floods, tornadoes, droughts, and earthquakes. It is hardly
sensible to say that the solar system is "indifferent" to
man's welfare; it is not even indifferent.

And so it is and has been with cultural systems. Although they have provided man with food and the fire
with which to cook it, huts and houses to protect him
from the elements, games and dances to entertain him,
gods and myths to beguile him, they have also slaught-
ered millions of men, women, and children in warfare, tor-
tured and killed them in inquisitions, or burned them to
death as witches. They have initiated or aggravated great
plagues by urban congestion and unsanitary practices.
The cultural systems brought into being and perpetuated
by the Agricultural Revolution reduced the majority of
mankind to slavery or serfdom, condemning them to a life
of labor, privation, and piety. The great era of civil socie-

ties—i.e., Civilization—subordinated human rights and values to property rights:

> Gold is the worst of ills that every plagued mankind; this wastes our cities, drives forth their natives to a foreign soil, taints the pure heart, and turns the virtuous mind to basest deeds; artificer of fraud supreme, the source of every wickedness (spoken by Creon, King of Thebes. Sophocles *Antigone* 260–65).

There is nothing, no crime however heinous, that will not be committed by someone, in civil societies, for money. Cultural systems have encouraged and rewarded the manufacture and sale of adulterated or contaminated food, and dangerous, even lethal, drugs. Culture put young children to work in textile mills for fifteen hours a day, begat sweat shops that consumed the lives of impecunious women who had no alternatives but starvation or prostitution. Modern cultures spawned the unspeakable almshouses where humanity was reduced to the ultimate of degradation.

As for making life secure and enduring for the human species, cultural systems have exterminated entire species of birds and animals that have served human needs. The arts of agriculture have rendered huge areas unfit for food production as a consequence of erosion, overgrazing, or salinification as a result of irrigation. The vast food resources of the oceans are threatened by contamination brought about by industrial and commercial practices. The atmosphere of the planet is being polluted by noxious gases. In short, cultural systems are moving rapidly to make the earth uninhabitable. And over all hovers the spector of annihilation by two lethal cultural devices: nuclear bombs and national sovereignty. Cultural systems, like stars and planets, are indifferent to the welfare—or the very existence—of man. The days when "the bad re-

volting stars consented to Henry's death" are gone forever.

This drastic change in my conception of culture
requires some explanation. My early conception was
formed when my primary concern was with primitive (preliterate) peoples: anthropology began as a focus upon the
preliterate and the prehistoric. I was impressed with the
qualities of "primitive society": it was based upon mutual
aid and cooperation; everyone had free access to the resources of nature; property rights were subordinated to
human rights and welfare. Primitive society was indeed
characterized by liberty, equality, and fraternity. I came to
regard culture as the benevolent custodian of mankind.

When I came to the Agricultural Revolution and its consequences I recognized that the institutions of primitive
society were extinguished and class structure and class
rule were established; property rights were elevated above
human rights and welfare (see Part Two: The Agricultural
Revolution and its Consequences in *The Evolution of Culture,* 1959b). But I did not revise my earlier conception of
culture. Perhaps I felt that the cruel and inhuman institutions of civil society were merely a temporary aberration,
and that the benevolent role of culture would eventually
be restored. Did not Morgan tell us, in a moving and elo-
quent passage toward the end of *Ancient Society* (p. 552
in the Holt edition), that "a mere property career is not the
final destiny of mankind. . . . Equality in rights and privileges. . . . foreshadow the next higher plane to which experience, intelligence and knowledge are steadily tending.
*It will be a revival, in a higher form, of the liberty, equality
and fraternity of the ancient gentes* [clans]" (emphasis
added). The perennial inspiration of Utopias has often
subverted a rational outlook.

What, then, is the function of culture? One must be
careful about the way he phrases a question; an inappro-

priate phrasing might be an obstacle to a meaningful answer. "What is the function of the earth?" for example, "the function of the solar system?" "What is the function of man?" I would not know how to answer these questions. But if we ask "What are the functions of this or that system?" we know how to proceed with an answer. Dictionaries tell us that a "function is the normal or characteristic action of anything" (*Websters* 1970); "the kind of action or activity proper to a person, thing, or institution" (*Random House* 1971). The function, or functions, of a system are the acts performed, the processes executed, by the system. We are now in a position to talk meaningfully about the functions of cultural systems.

systems in general

TO understand cultural systems in particular we must know something about systems in general. First, they are composed of interrelated, interdependent parts, or kinds of parts; these parts form the structure of the system. The parts interact with one another, and the system correlates and coordinates the parts to form an integral whole; these are the basic processes of all systems. Material systems (which includes cultural systems) are thermodynamic systems to which the laws of thermodynamics are applicable and illuminating. We distinguish three kinds of material systems: (1) systems in stable equilibrium in which the entropy* factor (energy and structure) is a constant or may be considered as a constant within certain limits, e.g., atoms of stable elements, the solar system (within our lifetime), some primitive (preliterate) bands; (2) systems moving in the direction of increasing entropy—increasing diffusion or dissipation of energy and greater disorder structurally, e.g., the cosmos ("The entropy of the world strives for a maximum"—Clausius), stars, radioactive terrestrial substances; and (3) systems moving in the direction of "negative entropy" (to borrow a term used by Erwin Schroedinger in *What Is Life?*, 1944 pp. 71–72, 75), i.e., greater concentration of energy and more complex structure, e.g., biological organisms and cultural systems (see White 1959b, chap. 2, "Energy and Tools").

Systems must be explained in terms of themselves, i.e., in terms of their respective structures

* Entropy: a thermodynamic measure of the amount of energy unavailable for useful work, and the degree of disorder, in a system.

and processes. To understand sugar we must concern ourselves with molecules of sugar; we cannot form a conception of sugar from an examination of its component atoms taken singly. We understand living cells in terms of themselves rather than their constituent molecules. A star becomes intelligible only when we consider it as a whole. Similarly, we must understand cultural systems in terms of their respective structures and processes, not in terms of human need, purpose, or act.

Cultural systems, like other kinds of material systems, exist in an environment; in actuality, no system exists in complete isolation. The interaction between a system and its environment affects the system in greater or lesser degree. The environment may hamper the functioning of a system; it may even destroy it. Or the environment may foster the functioning of the system. Or, finally, the environment may be neutral in its influence, tending neither to impede nor to foster the system's proper functions.

We distinguish two kinds of environments (or two significant facets of the environment) of cultural systems: (1) primates capable of articulate speech (symboling), and (2) the terrestrial and cosmic environment. The primates are significant as biological organisms, as animals. It is culture that transforms the primate into a human being. Human beings are embraced by and incorporated into cultural systems, but as bundles, or capsules, of culture; they are units of culture in primate form. They are the subjects of statistics—so many who drink coffee, vote, or go to ball games. All cultural systems are circumscribed by limits set by the intrinsic properties of their primate components: no cultural system could continue to exist that is so inimical to the incorporated primates that they become extinct. But to explain cultural systems in terms of "human nature" writ large is the grossest of misconceptions.* It is not human nature that produces culture; it is culture that puts the stamp of humanity upon a kind of primate. Helen Keller became a human being only after she and culture were brought together (see White 1969, pp. 36–39).

Cultural systems act and react upon one another, band with band, tribe with tribe, nations with tribes, and nations with nations. This interaction affects the systems themselves and tends to form new kinds of systems, such as tribal confederacies, nations, coalitions of nations, and world organizations. There have been two major types of cultural systems: the tribe and the state; each has subtypes. In the tribe category the spectrum runs from small and simply organized bands to large tribes with segmented structures and influential chiefs. The state has a number of varieties: the archaic state, feudalism, monarchy, the capitalist-democratic state, and the modern one-party communist state.

anatomy of cultural systems

It is convenient for purposes of exposition to analyze a cultural system into significant components: technological, sociological and ideological. Technology consists of tools and weapons and techniques of using them. Sociology includes customs, institutions, codes, etc. Ideology consists of ideas (concepts) and beliefs. All cultural systems are composed of these three classes of elements. They are, of course, interrelated; each is meaningful only in terms of its relationship to the other two, and to the system as a whole. The technological component, however,

* It is a sad commentary upon the intellectual culture of New England in the 19th century to recall that Emerson—"an institution is the lengthened shadow of one man"—was regarded as a brilliant and wise man by his contemporaries.

is the basic one; upon it social systems and ideologies—and cultural systems as a whole—depend.

Cultural systems, like all material systems, are thermodynamic systems. Their existence and operation require energy. Every cultural event—chipping an arrowhead, performing the duties of husband and father, performing a ritual or uttering a prayer—involves the expenditure of energy. It is the technological sector of a cultural system that harnesses and puts to use the energy necessary to the cultural system. It is the technological component that effects the articulation of a cultural system with its terrestrial habitat; upon the effectiveness of this articulation (adjustment) the existence of the cultural system depends.

Social systems and ideologies are functions of their technological bases; as the technology varies so will the social and ideological systems vary. Social organization may be meaningfully thought of as the way a people employs its technology in the two basic cultural processes: subsistence and defense/offense. Ideologies express the experience of the human carriers of culture as determined by technology and refracted through the medium of the social system. Just as a paleontologist can construct a species from a single molar tooth (Dr. Davidson Black and Sinanthropus), so can a culturologist picture a type of culture from one, or a few, basic elements of technology. A chipped stone implies the social organization of a band (a territorial group and families) and its mythology. Digging stick, hoe, and mortar and pestle indicate a horticultural mode of life upon a slightly higher plane than that of a band: a tribe, perhaps with clan organization, for example. A plow requires an ox, and together they point to field agriculture and the beginnings and subsequent development of literate, metallurgical cultures, with rulers, priests, and theology. The steam engine is the indicative feature of capitalism and representative government (democracy). The computer, intercontinental ballistic missiles, and interplanetary spacecraft bring us to still another stage of cultural development.

energy and cultural systems

In order to evolve, a biological or a cultural system must obtain energy in increasing quantities from the external world. In the process of evolving, these systems move in a direction opposite to that of the comos as a whole as specified by the Second Law of Thermodynamics: i.e., they move toward greater concentrations of energy and increasing structural complexity. The ultimate source of this energy is the sun although it is captured directly in this form by plants only (with insignificant exceptions in solar heated houses and spacecraft). Cultural systems first harnessed solar energy in the form of human beings; * subsequently fire, wind, and water provided energy for cultural development. The cultivation of plants marked a tremendous advance in the harnessing of solar energy. The domestication of animals, roughly contemporaneous with the development of agriculture, added further to the amount of energy made available for further development by cultural systems. The utilization of coal in steam engines, and petroleum and its derivatives in internal combustion engines, marked another step upward. Modern civilization has attained the threshold of the harnessing of nuclear energy. Cultural systems evolve (culture can evolve only in its systemic form) when and as the amount of energy per capita per year is increased, and as the efficiency of the tools and machines with which it is utilized is increased (White 1959b, chap. 2, "Energy and Tools").

* The conventional "man harnessed energy" is anthropocentric. As an explanatory device it is no better than "God did it." Anything that explains everything explains nothing.

The evolutionist process, in both the biological and cultural realms, is characterized by increase in magnitude of result, i.e., the multiplication of individual organisms, bands, and tribes, and by progressive differentiation of structure, i.e., the increase in the number of kinds of parts that make up the evolving systems. Differentiation of structure and specialization of function require ways and means to coordinate, regulate, and control the increasingly complex system.

Cultural systems grew out of subhuman primate societies. With the emergence of symboling, especially in the form of articulate speech, prehuman social organization and other forms of behavior were transformed into culture, which, once established, became a continuum that, as we have already noted, acquired a life of its own. Chapter 4 of *The Evolution of Culture,* "The Transition from Anthropoid Society to Human Society," will supplement the condensed sketch presented above. We now turn to cultural systems themselves.

cultural systems: structure and functions

Cultural systems, like all other kinds of systems, are made up of parts that are integrated into a coherent whole. Cultural systems, like all other kinds of systems, behave, i.e., they do things. Their behavior has two aspects: intrasystemic (within the system) and extrasystemic (reactions of the system to things lying outside itself). We may formulate a few basic generalizations that apply to all kinds of systems. Intrasystemic behavior is determined by the interaction of its constituent parts in terms of their intrinsic properties and in accordance with the principle of cause and effect. The extrasystemic behavior of a system is a function of the intrinsic properties of the system on the one hand, and of the thing reacted to, on the other. Intrinsic properties, interaction within the system, action and reaction between system and its environment, determinism, cause and effect: these are the concepts that make the behavior of systems intelligible to us. In effect, they say that an atom behaves like an atom; a cell, like a cell; a star or galaxy, like a star or galaxy; a mammal, like a mammal; a society of baboons, like a society of baboons; and a cultural system behaves like a cultural system.

It is self-evident that if a system is to persist it must do certain things: it must hold its parts together in a network of interrelationships and interdependence; it must subordinate part to whole; it must coordinate its parts and regulate the role of each, and finally it must exercise control over the system as a whole. We will leave to the reader to discover for himself how inanimate systems—atoms, stars, galaxies—are held together; and to learn from the biologist how single-celled organisms hold themselves together, and how multicellular organisms are integrated and controlled. We shall now proceed to an account of how cultural systems maintain themselves as systems.

As we have already noted, cultural systems emerged from the social systems of prehuman primates; it was the emergence of symboling in the course of neurological evolution that transformed prehuman primate society into human cultural systems. All forms of social organization, regardless of species, are determined by three factors: mode of subsistence, method of protection from enemies by defensive/offensive means, and method of reproduction (White 1959b, p. 11). The mode of subsistence of man's prehuman antecedents was conducive to group life and living together afforded them some protection from predators. Nonseasonal attraction between the sexes tended to form family groups, and the prolonged infancy of the offspring tended to bind generations together.

The first cultural systems contained the fundamentals of

the prehuman primate societies that preceded them—
local territorial groups and families. With regard to technology, the first human beings probably used some
tools/weapons; whether or not the use of tools had become habitual and traditional among man's immediate
prehuman ancestors is a question that is still under discussion. Ideologies in the sense in which we are using
that term (concepts and beliefs that can be transmitted by
means of articulate speech) were, of course, nonexistent
in the societies of man's prehuman antecedents. Prehuman primates may properly be said to have possessed
knowledge, however. We see no objection to saying that
these primates knew something about their habitats; they
certainly were able to distinguish the beneficial from the
injurious in many instances, otherwise they could not
have survived. Inasmuch as apes have demonstrated their
ability to use tools, including levers (White 1942), it seems
justified to say that they possessed knowledge in this area
also. If man's ancestors threw rocks at their enemies—as
according to some anthropologists they are supposed to
have done—one might say that they possessed a rudimentary understanding of ballistics.

The "institutions," habits, and knowledge that the first
human beings took over from their prehuman antecedents
were important, but they were crude, simple, and meager.
And, without articulate speech, the possibility of progress
on a merely primate level seems to have been extremely
limited if, indeed, it existed at all. It was symboling—par-
ticularly articulate speech—that changed all this: it
created cultural systems and launched them upon a
course of development. In the Word was the Beginning.

Without articulate speech *human* social organization
would be impossible. Codes of law, ethics, and etiquette
would be impossible. Without speech there could be no

mythologies and theologies, no gods to worship, no hells to go to. Even the technological process among primates was transformed by symboling (White 1942).*

kinship structure

The first specific innovative use of articulate speech was the creation of a *human* (i.e., dependent upon symboling) form of social organization. This form consisted of classifying all members of the group (band, or horde) in terms of kinship, i.e., parents, cousins, etc. Any society of primates is, of course, a network of biological relationships. But to every biological relationship there is a corresponding social relationship. In prehuman primate society these would be sociosexual relationships, mates, parents/offspring, relationships of dominance, subordination, etc. it was upon this network of social relationships that the first human societies were constructed.

There is less than general agreement among anthropologists with regard to the proposition that in primordial times people did not understand the biological process of reproduction; specifically, that they did not understand that copulation is the cause of pregnancy. I believe that it is highly probable that human society was organized upon the basis of genealogical social relationships long before the biological acts and processes of reproduction were understood.†

* Symboling and articulate speech are not synonymous; articulate speech is a particular form of symboling, the most important characteristic expression of this ability (see White 1962).

† It is easy for people in sophisticated societies to assume that the cause of pregnancy is fairly obvious, but this is not so. Given the primitive man's propensity to explain events in supernaturalistic terms (it might be assumed that a hunter who brings down a deer with his arrow could not have done so without magical aid), to believe that event *a* was caused by event *b*, which took place nine months previously, in the midst

Even with a full understanding of copulation and pregnancy, it would still be impossible to construct a human social system upon the basis of biological relationships because of the difficulty of determining these relationships in specific instances. Who is the father of the child has long been a pertinent question in human societies. "The father of the child is the husband of the mother" (Code Napoléon) is the closest that any culture has come to an answer to this question. But it is not necessary to know what the biological relationships are; it is the social relationship that counts. Our culture seems to have an obsession with biological relationships, real or assumed, but it holds that the mother of a child, in legal enactment and court decisions, is the woman who stands in a specified and legally sanctioned social relationship to the child regardless of who bore the child: legal adoption takes precedence over biological parenthood. In human societies, kinship is fundamentally sociological (culturological) rather than biological.

When certain primate groups had reached the threshold of symboling and crossed over to the life human, mere mating became marriage and offspring became "sons" and "daughters." The social relationships, both lineal and collateral, emanating from this primordial family were given names: husband, mother, child, cousin, etc. Families intermarried, thereby extending kinship ties to the boundaries of the band or horde: every individual became related to every other individual in a network of kinship ties that embraced the entire band.

These kinship relationships involved much more than genealogy (genealogy may be social as well as biological); they were also codes of behavior, specifying the duties

---

of hundreds of other events that might have been the cause, is placing a heavy burden upon the perspicacity of primitive man. In our society today it seems to be necessary to have courses in sex education.

and rights, the obligations and privileges of one relative to another. Society was thus organized upon the basis of kinship throughout the greater part of man's career as a human being; the kinship basis was overthrown by the Agricultural Revolution and the advent of civil societies (see chap. 6, "Kinship" and chap. 12, "The Agricultural Revolution" in White 1959b).

We return now to the question, Who did all this? Or, more to the point, How is the organization of human society upon the basis of named kinship ties to be explained? The traditional explanation is the anthropocentric one: "Why, people did it, of course." But *how* do people do this, if people are regarded as the causative agent, the explanatory device? Did some aboriginal genius originate the plan and persuade his fellows to adopt it? Or did they get together in groups ("committees") to work out a plan of organization? What evidence could be adduced in support of these explanations—except the existence of the societies and their kinship systems?

An ethnographer who has had firsthand experience with preliterate societies, such as an American Indian tribe, would, I believe, find the suggestion of a preliterate Solon or a democratic legislative caucus a bit absurd. These societies, based upon kinship ties, had much that requires explanation: their kinship terminology, for example. This was a special golssary of kinship terms that organized individuals into coherent societies and made effective conduct of social life possible.

The classificatory system of relationship, which merged lineal and collateral kin at certain points (father's brother becomes "father," father's sister's son may become "father," parallel cousins become "brothers" and "sisters," etc.), was "invented" in primordial times and used as long as tribal societies existed. The very existence of classificatory systems of kinship terminology was not discovered by scholars until the second half of the nineteenth century. * And its intricacies have not yet been explained to the satisfaction of anthropologists. If the Chinese were not aware of the tonal structure of their language until after they had possessed civilization for two thousand years, as Kroeber (1944, p. 224) has told us, how could eolithic savages be expected to have understood these kinship systems, or to have been aware that they were classificatory? Anthropocentric, psychological explanations simply do not explain; ethnological problems cannot be solved by introspection.

A culturological explanation can illuminate and make intelligible the origin of the classificatory system of relationship: we begin by applying to our problem the thesis that explanation consists of observing the behavior of things (in this case, cultural elements) in terms of their intrinsic properties and in terms of the principle of cause and effect.

We begin with a more or less enduring relationship between a man and a woman, inherited from prehuman antecedents. The transformation of mating to marriage originates new concepts and new terms: marriage, husband, wife. A child is born to the husband-wife couple; no understanding of the nature of copulation is required. An-

* The first discovery of the classificatory system of relationship was made by Joseph Francois Lafitau (1670–1746), a French Jesuit missionary among the Iroquois of Canada (1712–1717). He appears to have understood it quite well. He included an account of it in his *Moers des sauvages Ameriquains, comparees aux moers des premiers temps* (Paris, 1724). But Lafitau's discovery remained unnoted by anthropologists until 1889 when Edward Burnett Tylor brought it to their attention in his significant essay, "On a Method of Investigating the Development of Institutions; Applied to Laws of Marriage and Descent" (1889, p. 261). It was Lewis H. Morgan whose independent discovery of the classificatory system made it known—and intelligible—to the scientific world (see White 1957; see also 1964).

other social relationship becomes conceptualized and expressed in a word: child—son or daughter. Another child is born and a new relationship is recognized and conceptualized: sibling—brother or sister. And so it goes until the various social relationships in the ramification of genealogy, lineal and collateral, have been named: grandparent, uncle, aunt, nephew, niece, cousin, grandchild, etc.

The "classificatory" feature of kinship systems of preliterate peoples is explained sociologically. Father's brother is called "father" because his *social* relationship to the person speaking (conventionally referred to as "ego" by students of kinship terminologies) is of the *same kind* as the social relationship of father. The same applies to mother. A person may, of course, have only one mother biologically; but he may have several "mothers" sociologically. The social relationship between *ego* and his parallel cousins may be, and often is, the same as the social relationship between *ego* and his own siblings; they are, therefore, called "brother" and "sister." In one form of the classificatory system, a man's father's sister's son is called "father"; so also is father's sister's daughter's son—and father's sister's daughter's daughter's son. Why? Because they are all males in *ego's* father's matrilineal lineage.

The system of kinship terminology begins with the nuclear family, then extends outwards, collaterally and lineally, embracing ties established by marriage as well as those established by reproduction, until everyone in the society is embraced by a single network of kinship ties. This is a significant step in the process of system building. The social system from which human society emerged was a very loosely constructed system: a troop of prehuman primates. It had very little internal structure; the strongest ties were those of sexual unions and those between mothers and offspring; the former was rather precarious, the latter would soon be outgrown. The cohesiveness of the troop was not very great. The creation of a verbal device for naming and classifying all individuals in the society was accompanied by specified codes of behavior governing each kind of relationship: each person had certain rights and privileges, and duties and obligations, with reference to individuals in each kind of relationship (we shall return to this point later). In this way the society was given a complex internal structure—a "web of kinship"—that gave the society much greater cohesiveness than the societies of prehuman primates. A stronger, more powerful system was thus created and established.

prohibition of incest

Simultaneously with the origin of a kinship terminology, another event of the greatest importance took place—the definition and prohibition of incest.

Incest has had a curious fascination for the inhabitants of Western culture, from Sophocles' *Oedipus Rex* (fifth century B.C.) to Eugene O'Neil's *Desire Under the Elms* (1924). The scientific literature on the subject is voluminous, but few theories have come close to a satisfactory explanation of the origin of the incest taboo; some scholars have virtually given up the quest in despair. The failure of most attempts to solve the problem has been due to the fact that it has been approached from a psychological point of view, whereas the origin is not a psychological problem, but a culturological one. Another difficulty has been the confusion of *incest* with *inbreeding*. These concepts are not identical by any means; the brother-sister marriages in the ruling families of ancient Egypt, Peru, and Hawaii were not instances of incest but of an intensification of endogamy. Incest is, by definition, a crime: a sexual or marriage union between individuals who stand in a prohibited degree of relationship to each other. Definitions of "prohibited degrees of relationship" vary widely. Thus, in some aboriginal Australian tribes it would be incestuous for a man to marry his first parallel cousin, but he is not only permitted, but is required, to marry a first cross-cousin. Or, in another culture it would be incestous to marry a 64th cousin who was a member of one's own clan, but marriage with a first cousin in a clan not one's own would be permissible. *

The concept of cultural systems helps us to formulate an illuminating and satisfying theory of the definition and prohibition of incest (note that incest cannot be prohibited until it has been defined). Incest was defined and rules to prevent or punish the commission of incest were established in order to require interfamilial marriage and to prevent intrafamilial marriage (the question of brother-sister marriage did not come up until hundreds of thou-

* The confusion of incest with inbreeding in modern anthropological literature is extensive and a bit distressing. Incest is defined as something that is prohibited, as a crime, by *Webster's New International Dictionary,* 3d ed., and by the *Oxford English Dictionary.* But we find anthropologists and sociologists speaking of "royal incest," or "permissive incest." "There was royal incest in Egypt and in Hawaii . . ." i.e., brother-sister marriage (Fortune 1932, p. 622). Similarly, Lowie (1934, p. 233) speaks of "Peruvian and Hawaiian incest." B. Z. Seligman speaks of "the privilege to form incestuous unions" (1929, p. 254), and ". . . where incest is allowed" (1950a, p. 314). *Notes and Queries on Anthropology,* edited for the British Association for the Advancement of Science (5th ed., 1929), defines incest as "sexual intercourse between prohibited degrees of kindred" (p. 93). But, on the very next page there is a discussion captioned: "Legalized Incestuous Marriage."

The confusion and error of the scholars quoted above derive, no doubt, from the belief, or feeling, that incest *is* something in and of itself—just as other anthropologists tell us what culture "basically is." Again, Adam called the equine beast a horse because it *was* a horse. Incest is that which is called, defined as; incest—and incest is defined as a crime. The difference between incest and inbreeding is similar to the distinction between murder and homicide (see White's letter to the editor of *MAN,* 1958).

sands of years later). This was done because interfamilial marriage promoted the formation of the all-embracing web of kinship, providing society with connective tissue among all family groups, thereby increasing the cohesiveness of the society and the strength and power of the cultural system.

More or less durable sexual-social unions existed in the societies of man's prehuman ancestors. These unions, together with their infant offspring, constituted families. But the sexual-social unions were not substantial; they were subject to disruption at any time from a variety of causes. More important, however, was the fact that families formed by these unions were isolated; they were not related to one another by nonbiological ties; they were not integrated to form a social system.

In an article, "The Incest Taboo and the Mating Patterns of Animals," a group of scholars (Aberle et al., 1963) stated that "the social and cultural system theory [of the origin of the incest taboo] . . . requires that primitive men understand the advantages of the exchange [i.e., interfamilial marriage]—or else must assume that familial exogamy and the familial taboo arose as a chance 'mutation' and survived because of their adaptive character" (p. 258).

This is precisely what the culturological theory does *not* require; on the contrary, it shows why primitive men did not understand the origin of the incest taboo. Culturological theory argues that it was not *people* who originated the taboo—that is, it was not the work of a *neurological* system—but that it was the *cultural* system that produced it. So powerful still is the anthropocentric philosophy that it is often impossible, even for professional scientists, to conceive of any kind of causation or explanation other than the anthropocentric one; explanation is arrived at by introspection, i.e., outside the scope of science.

Even in the society of man's immediate nonhuman ancestors, society, the social system, did things, i.e., caused events to occur that could not have been produced by an individual as an individual. This capability became much more powerful when human society emerged.

In the prehuman primate family there were both endogamous and exogamous tendencies (forces). There was a tendency for parents to have sexual intercourse with their offspring as a part of the intimate social relationship between them. Exogamy was effected by the father expelling from the family a maturing male offspring because he threatened the monopoly of the female members enjoyed by the male parent. The prehuman primate family contained both integrative and disintegrative tendencies. An effective social or cultural system could not be constructed as long as the family groups were autonomous and endogamously inclined, i.e., as long as familial anarchy prevailed.

If a system, biological or cultural, possesses energy resources beyond the necessity of merely maintaining the status quo, it will evolve, i.e., take steps to produce a more highly organized, more powerful system. The earliest human societies possessed sufficient energy resources (supplied by the human-capsule carriers of culture) to evolve to a higher level of integration. The steps taken were the definition and prohibition of incest, which banned intrafamiliar marriage, making interfamilial marriage obligatory. The extension of interfamilial marriage eventually integrated all families of the tribe into a single network of consanguinity and affinity. Thus, a new kind of social organization was erected upon the firm basis of prehuman primate sexual unions.

Individuals were not likely to prohibit intrafamiliar sexual unions. The tendency to have sexual relations with an intimate associate is a powerful primate urge. "How oft it chances that in dreams a man has wed his mother" (spoken by Jocasta. Sophocles *Oedipus Rex* 981). Many psychiatrists believe that an incestuous wish is at the root of most neuroses. Far from being the work of individuals, the incest taboo was a blow struck against the individual: "the prohibition against incestuous object-choice [was] perhaps the most maiming wound ever inflicted . . . on the erotic life of man," in the opinion of Sigmund Freud (1930, p. 74). To say that "man" prohibited incest because it was wrong is, of course, nonsense; acts are not prohibited because they are wrong; they become wrong upon being prohibited (e.g., the Volstead Act).

The prohibition of incest is the first identifiable act in human history. It is the first instance of the subordination of the desire of the individual to the common good. As such, it is the first ethical act of history. The incest taboo marks the beginning of human social evolution. Had not interfamiliar marriage unions been made mandatory, social evolution would have been impossible.

The foregoing theory receives support from facts pertaining to the punishment meted out to offenders. The incest taboo is found on the lowest known levels of cultural development. It was almost invariably punished by death. The reason was that incest was a blow struck at the very foundations of human society in the early stages of its development. Punishment for the commission of incest today in our culture is very light because it is no longer a blow struck at the foundation of our culture. Breaking-and-entering and stealing and robbing banks are, however, blows struck at the foundation of our cultural system and are punished accordingly.

We must not leave the subject of incest without recognizing the contribution made by E. B. Tylor, who offered to anthropologists the key to an understanding of this great event. * In his notable essay "On a Method of Investigating the Development of Institutions; Applied to Laws of Marriage and Descent", he observed that "again and again in the world's history, savage tribes have had plainly before their minds the simple practical alternative between marrying-out and being killed-out" (1889, p. 267).

Tylor may be pardoned for indulging in psychological explanation in 1889. He is sound in seeing being killed-out as an alternative to marrying-out. But he errs in locating this perception in the mind of "savages" instead of cultural systems—those "complex wholes" about which he had written elsewhere with insight and understanding.

Tylor's key to an understanding of the origin of the incest taboo was not recognized by anthropologists in general. A. L. Kroeber and T. T. Waterman included Tylor's essay "On a Method . . ." in their *Source Book in Anthropology* (1920). Some years later (1931) when they prepared a new edition they abridged Tylor's essay, ostensibly to save space, and left out this precious key!

how can a cultural system "do" something?

Students have often asked, "How can a cultural system *do* something? Isn't it *people* who do this and that?" Their query is justified in the light of much that they derive from their teachers: "Empire-building is done not by 'nations' but by men" (Moon 1926, p. 58). "The forces that bring about the changes are active in the individuals composing the social group, not in the abstract culture. . . . It seems hardly necessary," said Franz Boas, "to consider culture a mystic entity that exists outside the society of its individ-

---

* 1400 years before Tylor, St. Augustine discussed the reasons for exogamy and, indirectly, the prohibition of incest in an illuminating way in *The City of God,* bk. 15.

ual carriers, and that moves by its own force" (1928, p. 236).

To say that "culture patterns . . . can act upon an individual is as absurd as to hold a quadratic equation capable of committing a murder" (Radcliffe-Brown 1957, p. 30). But Émile Durkheim, who is generally supposed to have been Radcliffe-Brown's model and inspiration, holds that culture can cause people to commit suicide: "Collective tendencies [i.e., culture] have an existence of their own; they are forces as real as cosmic forces . . . they likewise affect the individual from without. Moral acts such as suicide . . . depend on forces external to the individual . . . the stable number of suicides can only be due to the influence of a common cause which dominates and survives the individual" (1951, pp. 309, 313). And, of course, we are familiar with instances of Japanese disembowelling themselves, or Westerners blowing out their brains with a hand gun, to wipe out a stain of dishonor.

"The individual alone is real: neither society nor group is imbued with genuine unity" (Georg Simmel, in Vierkandt 1934, p. 61). "It is always the individual that really thinks and acts and revolts" (Sapir 1917, p. 442). * And, of course, the classic pronouncement of Robert S. Lynd: "culture does not enamel its fingernails, or vote, or believe in capitalism, but people do" (1939, p. 22). Thus, the fair flowers of the hardy perennials of anthropocentrism.

The proposition that "culture is an abstraction" has been widely held—by Kroeber and Kluckhohn (1952 passim), by Beals and Hoijer (1953, p. 210), by Robert Redfield (1941, p. 132), and by many others. Culture is viewed

---

* "It is this aggregation which thinks, feels, and wills. . . ." The social aggregate "in its totality . . . is that which thinks, feels, wishes" (Durkheim 1953 [1898], p. 26.)

"Who is it who feels, thinks, tastes; not the individual but the social group," Gumplowicz 1899, p. 158; see also p. 157.

as "a logical construct" by Kroeber and Kluckhohn (1952, p. 189), as "something of a statistical fiction," by Edward Sapir (1932, p. 237). It is not surprising, therefore, that the logical conclusion of this line of reasoning, that "culture has no ontological reality" (Spiro 1951, p. 24), was eventually reached. How a science—non-biological (i.e., cultural) anthropology—could function without a real subject matter was a question that no one asked and that seemed to disturb no one. But try to imagine a science of mammalogy functioning with unreal foxes, abstract cows, and fictitious bears.

There have been a few explicit exceptions to the "culture is not real" thesis. Julian Huxley (1955, pp. 15–16) wrote: "If anthropology is to be a science, then for anthropologists culture must be defined, not philosophically or metaphysically, nor as an abstraction, . . . but as something which can be investigated by the methods of scientific inquiry, a phenomenal process occurring in space and time." And Frederica De Laguna (1968, p. 475), in her presidential address to the AAA, views culture "as a natural phenomenon of the natural world."

"Culture is a concept; a concept is an abstraction; abstractions are not perceptible; therefore culture is not real." Something like this seems to have been the line of reasoning that has led some anthropologists to become mired in a semantic tar pit. David Bidney (1954, p. 459) has clarified this situation: "They have confused the *concept of culture,* which is a logical construct, with the *actual, existential culture,* which is a distinctively human mode of living and acting" (emphases added). Of course, *culture* is a concept. So, also, *fox* is a concept. But the *concept* "fox" is one thing; the little bushy-tailed animal is something else. The concept "fox" is meaningful only because it corresponds to something real in the external world; in the realm of time and space, as Huxley put it. So it is with culture: the concept is empty and meaningless without real things and events in terrestrial time and space.

It is little wonder if students find it difficult to see how a "logical construct" or a "statistical fiction" can do something. Fortunately, we have something more substantial to offer them. First of all, let us direct their attention to some noncultural systems, and ask the same question, "How can they do anything?" Or, to put the question specifically, "What kind of behavior does the system in question exhibit, and how is said behavior to be explained?" Take the solar system, for example. We observe planets revolving around the central body, the sun; satellites revolve around some of the planets. How is the solar system able to do what it does? is a rather senseless question today. But formerly this was not the case: "God created the sun, the moon and the stars and set them in motion in their courses." How can a hen (a system) lay an egg? How can a cow (a system) produce milk? How can a snowflake (a system) form itself? How can culture (a cultural system) cause a man to kill himself?

The old theological, and later the anthropocentric, way of looking at things and events in the world we live in still persists, even in the social sciences. There must be some intelligent, purposeful being behind the phenomenal world. "The sun is trying to come out." Our language is so structured as to require a subject for every act: "It rains."

If culture must be explained in cultural terms, as anthropologists noted above have argued, then cultural systems must be explained in terms of themselves, in terms of their components, their structure. They are explained in terms of the intrinsic properties of their components and the integration of these parts in a unity—all in accordance with the principle of cause and effect. This is the way we explain how the various systems we have cited as examples—the solar system, the hen, the cow, the snow-flake—can "do the things that they do," i.e., how and why they behave as they do. Finally, we are brought to the realization that "man" or "people" is not an explanatory device. To say that it is *people* who define and prohibit incest, originate classificatory systems of kinship terminology, and establish institutions of feudalism or capitalism is merely to say that culture cannot exist without people, a proposition that no one, least of all culturologists, would deny.

Of course it is people, not cultural systems, who swallow aspirin tablets. But this is not the point at issue. The question is, *why* do they take aspirin instead of resorting to charms, spells, or prayers to cure themselves of an ailment? Furthermore, how do they come to have aspirin instead of fetishes?

We have already shown by the aid of the concept of cultural system how and why the classificatory system of relationship and the definition and prohibition of incest were achieved. The problem of their origins could not have been solved without this concept. We shall now proceed to other problems which have been similarly solved.

the generation of ethical codes

ETHICAL codes originated with the definition and prohibition of incest; here was the first identifiable "Thou shall not . . ." in human history. To ascribe ethical codes to an eolithic genius or a convention of savages is, perhaps, an advance over the biblical account of the fruit of the tree in Eden that endowed Adam and Eve with a knowledge of good and evil, or of Moses descending Mount Sinai with the Commandments of Jehovah engraved on tablets of stone, but it leaves much to be desired. Ethical codes were the work of cultural systems.

It is commonly believed that ethical codes have to do with good and evil, and with commandments and exhortation to cause people to do good deeds and to refrain from evil ones. This conception is sound as far as it goes, but it does not go far enough. Ethical codes require people to promote the welfare—or what is deemed to be the welfare—of society. This action, like refraining from committing incest, requires the subordination of the individual (the part) to society (the whole). The cultural system is the whole. The parts are capsules of culture in human form. Definitions of the good, like definitions of incest, vary from culture to culture. But whatever the definition, each cultural system requires its human components to work toward common goals. The effect of ethical codes is to produce unity and harmony of human conduct in the interest of the system as a whole. Cultural systems are thus made more stable, more harmonious, and therefore more effective in the conduct of their internal behavior and more powerful in their competition with other cultural systems.

Human beings are the only objects in the world to which the concepts of good and bad are relevant. It is this fact that makes it possible for cultural systems to manipulate and control human beings as components of cultural systems. So powerful is the response of the talking primate to the stimuli of The Good that they are willing to suffer and die for the particular good that their cultural system holds before them. "Dying for one's country"—one of the most noble forms of death—is, therefore, dying for one's cultural system. This is one of the many things that a cultural system does to men. Conscience, Radcliffe-Brown (1934, p. 531) observed, "is the reflex in the individual of the sanctions of society." The "still small voice of conscience" thus turns out to be the command of a cultural system.

etiquette

In sharp contrast with the great preoccupation with ethics in Western culture, and the voluminous literature on the subject, is the meager concern with etiquette on the part of social scientists. It is as if etiquette were too trivial, too frivolous, to merit serious attention. Tables of contents of scores of anthropological and sociological treatises contain no reference to etiquette. *A Dictionary of the Social Sciences,* edited by Julius Gould and William L. Kolb (1964), contains no article on etiquette. The article on "Etiquette" in the *Encyclopaedia of the Social Sciences* (1934) gives numerous examples of the observance of rules of etiquette, but goes no further than to derive etiquette from ceremony and ritual, and since "ritual centers around divinity, so does etiquette" (p. 615). The author, anthropologist A. M. Hocart, does not comprehend the nature and function of etiquette.

Codes of etiquette are among the most important mechanisms of social regulation and control in any human society. Their purpose and function are to regulate the behavior of individuals so as to keep them in their proper class, thereby keeping the classes intact, thereby preserving the class structure, order, and stability of cultural systems.

All primate societies have class structures. We define a class as one of an indefinite number of parts of a society in which the composition of each part differs from the composition of the others. In prehuman primate society the classes are male, female, mated, nonmated, adult, etc. In the earliest human societies the basic classes were much the same as those of their anthropoid antecedents: married, single, widowed, adult, prepuberty youths, infants, the nonproductive aged, etc. But in addition to these were the numerous classes established by the classificatory system of relationship: fathers, mothers, siblings, children, cousins, etc. In more advanced cultures, classes of nobles, lords, priests, scribes, craftsmen, serfs, and slaves are found.

To simplify an account of the operation of a code of etiquette, it may be said that each class is distinguished by a kind of behavior and perhaps by dress or insignia. The rules of etiquette require each member of a class to behave, dress, speak, etc., as a member of his class. He must also behave in a specified manner to members of other classes. The code thus gives distinctiveness to each class and lays down the rules for the regulation of the social relations among classes. In these ways the class structure of society is defined, regulated, and preserved, giving order and stability to the cultural system of which it is a part. Furthermore, a code of etiquette and the observance of its rules make prediction of behavior possible, which contributes greatly to the effective functioning of the social system: the lord knows how to behave to the king, to other lords, and to serfs; the behavior of a college dean can be predicted within fairly narrow limits, as can that of an American politician running for office, a traffic cop, a Catholic priest, etc. Without the possibility of reliable predictions the orderly and effective conduct of social life would be all but impossible.

exogamy/endogamy

There has been much lack of understanding concerning these two concepts. With regard to the origin of the former, E. B. Tylor (1889, p. 267) wrote: "Exogamy lies far back in the history of man, and perhaps no observer has ever seen it come into existence, nor have the precise conditions of its origin yet been clearly inferred." In *Totemism and Exogamy* (1910, 1: 165) Sir James G. Fraser observed: "Thus the ultimate origin of exogamy, and with it of the law of incest—since exogamy was devised to prevent incest—remains a problem nearly as dark as ever. All that seems fairly probable is that both of them originated in a savage superstition, to which we have lost the clue." Brenda Seligman (1929, p. 238) regards "exogamy . . . [as] a factor of premier importance, but one whose functional nature is unknown."

It has been believed that a culture may or may not practice exogamy: "in cultures where exogamy is practiced and in those where there is no trace of the custom" (Seligman 1950a, p. 314); "the Andean region lacks . . . exogamy" (Lowie 1940, p. 412). Some writers give the impression that exogamy flourishes in preliterate cultures, but that endogamy is "rare" (Wedgwood, 1929). "Endogamy flourishes in stratified societies," says Lowie (1933), "and is illustrated in the royal marriages of modern Europe and in the prevalent inbreeding of its aristocracies." But, some scholars say "exogamy and endogamy are by no means mutually exclusive" (Wedgwood, 1929). Lowie observes that "exogamy and endogamy are not mutually exclusive except with regard to the same unit" (1920, p. 17)—which of course would be impossible. It is obvious that the understanding of these authors is rather limited.

It is rather discouraging to note that among anthropologists, the clearest understanding of exogamy and endogamy is to be found almost a century ago in the writings of E. B. Tylor. His understanding is limited and at points outdated: he sees a significant relationship between exogamy and the practice of "wife capture" (1889, p. 265). But he views them as correlative processes: "On looking at the distinction between endogamy and exogamy . . . it will be seen that there is a period in the growth of society when it is a political question of the first importance . . . endogamy is a policy of isolation. . . ." (1889, p. 267) whereas exogamy is a practice of expansion and consolidation.

The reason why so many otherwise astute observers have failed to understand the full significance of endogamy and exogamy, I venture to suggest, is that they lacked (or did not use in their interpretations) the concept of cultural system. Tylor comes closer to this conception than other writers cited.

All material systems are characterized by two opposite but inseparable and complementary processes: inward-moving and outward-moving, centripetal and centrifugal; plus and minus expressions of electromagnetic behavior. Endogamy and exogamy are the names of these processes with reference to marriage in human social systems.

In the earliest human social systems the family was the basic unit. Standing alone, the family was weak. A social system where families were independent and autonomous would be a weak system; from the standpoint of integration it would resemble a colony of unicellular organisms. The classificatory system of relationship brought all families together in a strong network of social ties. This system involved much more than the relations of consanguinity and affinity, however; it contained a code of ethics that endowed each kinship tie with mutual or correlative duties and obligations, thus regulating the behavior of every individual toward his kindred. The code of ethics was accompanied by a code of etiquette that regulated social intercourse. And, finally and most importantly the kinship was an economic system, a system of mutual aid and cooperation, a system in which human welfare was placed above property rights. Kinship organization taken as a whole made tribal society close-knit, highly integrated (although on a low level of cultural development), and effective in the conduct of life within the tribe and in its relations with neighboring tribes. And exogamy and endogamy played an important role in the creation of this kind of society. Tylor said this clearly in 1889 when he wrote: "Endogamy is a policy of isolation, cutting off a horde or village, even from the parent-stock whence it separated. . . . Exogamy, enabling a growing tribe to keep itself compact by constant unions between its spreading clans, enables it to overmatch any number of small intermarrying groups, isolated and helpless" (p. 267) (Tylor's terminology should not be permitted to obscure the point he is making). And again: "Exogamy thus shows itself as an institution which resists the tendency of uncultured populations to disintegrate, cementing them into nations [tribes] capable of living together in peace and holding together in war until they reach the period of higher military and political organization" (p. 268).

Exogamy operates to form larger cooperative groups of individuals bound together by the ties of consanguinity and affinity. And, other factors being constant, a larger group would be more effective than a smaller one in the fundamental activities of subsistence and defense-offense. But another significant factor is involved here also—solidarity. The effectiveness of a social group is a function of its size (i.e., the number of individuals contained in it), and of its solidarity (i.e., the cohesiveness, the intensity of the ties that bind one individual to another). These factors are opposed to each other in their influence. Increase in size would tend to diminish the solidarity of the group. An increase of solidarity would tend to diminish the size of the group. Thus, to obtain maximum effectiveness of the social group, a balance between the factors of size and solidarity must be achieved. This is precisely what the laws of exogamy and endogamy accomplish. Thus, the processes (or "laws") of exogamy and endogamy operate like a thermostat in a heated house: if the temperature falls below a certain point, the thermostat turns on the furnace; if the temperature rises above a certain point, the thermostat turns off the furnace. The correlative action of the processes of exogamy and endogamy within a cultural system is one of the most ingenious devices in the history of culture. The notion that primitive men "must have understood" these processes in order to bring about their correlative operation is less than reasonable inasmuch as many students of culture today do not understand the processes of exogamy and endogamy taken singly, to say nothing of comprehending their correlative position in cultural systems. This lack of understanding, it should be noted, is due almost entirely to the absence of the concept of cultural system. Once one sees exogamy and endogamy not merely as "marrying out" and "marrying in," but observes them in their relationship to the cultural system of which they are processes, it becomes possible to understand them in their relationship to each other and to the cultural system as a whole.

Because of his conception of culture as "a complex whole," Tylor had been almost alone in his understanding of exogamy/endogamy until the early 1930s when A. R. Radcliffe-Brown gave evidence of a similar understanding:

"In any society there are normally present a certain number of factors tending towards an expansion of social solidarity, and other factors tending in the opposite direction towards a contraction of social solidarity" (1931b, p. 445). Radcliffe-Brown does not mention the factor of size in the passage above, but elsewhere he points out that the transition from the Kariera system of relationship to the Aranda system in aboriginal Australia produced a larger kinship grouping:

"In terms of hordes the marriage system of the Aranda type results in a more complex integration than the Kariera system, linking an individual to four hordes in all [instead of only two as in the Kariera system]. [In the Aranda system, the four hordes are] first his own, i.e., his father's . . . secondly his mother's . . . his mother's brother's horde, [and the horde of his mother's mother's brother, whose daughter is the mother of his wife]" (1931b, p. 451).

Prohibition of unions defined as incestuous began with the family: marriage, or sexual unions, between parents and children and between brother and sister. But, since endogamous processes were correlated with exogamous processes, when one union was prohibited, another was required to achieve the optimum balance between these two processes. We may infer, on the basis of our theory, that when marriage with a sibling was prohibited, marriage with the next closest relative would be required. This relative would be a parallel cousin, inasmuch as the "social distance" between parallel cousins is less than the distance between cross-cousins. When marriage between parallel cousins was no longer conducive to the maximum effectiveness of the group, this union was prohibited and marriage with first cross-cousins was required. We know, of course, that cross-cousin marriage was a widespread institution among peoples on lower levels of cultural development. In aboriginal Australia we have evidence of the prohibition of marriage with a first cross-cousin (a male marrying his mother's brother's daughter) and marriage with a second cross-cousin (a male marrying his mother's mother's brother's daughter's daughter) as in the transition from the Kariera system to the Aranda system, noted above.

Usually, however, when marriage with a first cross-cousin is prohibited, the endogamous process requires marriage, not with someone standing in a particular genealogical relationship, but with someone who is a member of another group, such as a moiety, or with a person who is a member of any clan except one's own (White 1959b, pp. 105–11).

Exogamous and endogamous processes (customs, rules) exist upon advanced cultural levels as well as upon lower levels. Aristocratic classes tend to be endogamous. Many religious and ethnic groups strive to maintain endogamy, while observing the rules of exogamy within their own respective groups. There is a tendency in modern Western culture for the wealthy class to practice endogamy although an explicit rule to this effect may not be evident. Many states of the United States have had laws prohibiting interracial marriage, which has had the effect of requiring one to marry within his own race.

Thus we see that the definition and prohibition of incestuous unions, and the operation of the correlative processes of endogamy/exogamy, are processes of cultural systems and can be fully understood only as such.

segmentation

We define "segment" as one of an indefinite number of like parts that compose a system. We find segmental organization wherever we look. Galaxies are segments of the universe; star clusters may be segments within a galaxy. Atoms are segments of molecules; molecules are segments of a mass of an element—carbon, lead, etc. A cell is a segment of living tissue. Many biological organisms are segmented, e.g., worms, crayfish. Cultural systems are characterized by segmentation from the lowest levels of development to the highest. In preliterate cultural systems we find families, lineages, clans, tribes (within a confederacy), etc. Civil societies are segmented into nomes and provinces; cities are composed of demes, wards, or barrios. Various institutions in civil societies are segmented, such as military and ecclesiastical organizations.

An understanding of the processes of endogamy and exogamy helps us to understand segmentation. The function of segmentation is to make possible an increase in size of a system without suffering a diminution of solidarity. It does this in two ways: (1) by intensifying the cohesion of the components of a segment, such as the individual members of a clan (expressed by the word "clannish"), and (2) by establishing and fortifying the cohesion of the segments within the system as a whole. An army of 30,000 men would be virtually unmanageable and useless. But segmented, it can become powerful and effective: cohesion, solidarity, is established within and among its segments—companies, battalions, regiments, brigades, divisions, etc., on up the stratified structure to its top. Large church organizations derive their unity, their solidarity, and their effectiveness as organizations from the cohesiveness of the stratified series of segments: congregations, parishes, bishoprics, archdioceses, etc.

lineal segmentation in preliterate societies

The tie between parents and children is, of course, a powerful one, perhaps the most powerful and enduring tie in human society. The continuity of parent-child relationships forms lineages. At first they are merely de facto groupings. As they increase in importance they are socially recognized, receive names, and become exogamous. Descent may be reckoned matrilineally, or patrilineally, or ambilineally. A society may recognize only two lines of descent; the groups thus formed are called (by ethnologists) *moieties.* If an indefinite number of lineages are recognized, they are called *clans.* Moieties are either patrilineal or matrilineal and are exogamous. In a system of matrilineal descent, I would belong to my mother's moiety, my parallel cousins would belong to my moiety, my cross-cousins to my father's moiety. I must marry a cross-cousin (if I do marry); I cannot marry a parallel cousin because she would be my sibling, i.e., designated as "sister." The division of the tribe into two exogamous parts is a way of intensifying the solidarity of the tribe: first within the moiety and second by the obligation of moieties to intermarry.

Some tribes with moieties have clan organizations also, each moiety being composed of segments. This results in the fostering of clan solidarity within the moiety as well as in the tribe as a consequence of intermarriage between the moieties. Some tribes have clans but not moieties. Clans and moieties are thus seen to be integral parts of an evolving social system, as the social system is a part of the cultural system as a whole.

The emergence of clan organization in the social evolutionary process is thus made clear and intelligible. We do not find this understanding in American ethnology, however. For decades ethnology has not provided an adequate answer to the question, "How has clan organization come into existence?" This has been due in part to the negative attitude toward cultural evolutionist theory, and in large part to a lack of understanding of the process of segmentation. For decades in American ethnology the presence of clans in specific tribes has been attributed to diffusion: tribe A has borrowed clan organization from tribe B; if a tribe is without clans it is because it has not borrowed them from a neighbor. This was the prevailing view in American ethnology during the closing years of the nineteenth century and for some decades in the twentieth century.

But clan organization cannot diffuse unless it is already in existence. How did clans originate in the first place? Few ethnologists have ventured explanations. Franz Boas speaks of a "psychic factor" that "molded" both clans and secret societies (1897, pp. 660–61), and of "psychic conditions" that favored the existence of totemic organization of society (1896, p. 903). This explanation is little better than the old explanation of the origin of fossils: they were formed by "the congelation of lapidific juices." Malinowski (1929, p. 868b) said that "clans were originally magical bodies engaged in controlling, through spell and rite, certain animal or vegetable species for the welfare of the tribe." Radcliffe-Brown (1931b, p. 441) invoked "a universal sociological law though it is not yet possible to formulate precisely its scope, namely, a society has need to provide itself with a segmentary [clan] organization." I believe he was on the right track, but he certainly fell far short of an explanation of the origin of clans: "need" is not enough. Julian Steward (1937) was more realistic. He cogently argued that clan organization was brought about by the operation of significant factors in the way of life of a people, such as mode of subsistence, density of population, customs of residence, etc.

The position of Boasian ethnology with regard to the presence or absence of clan organization among certain tribes or within certain regions is rather curious. As early as 1896 Boas wrote: "There can be no doubt that this form of social organization [clans which have totems] has arisen independently over and over again" (1896, p. 903). In 1920 Lowie made a remarkable statement that was, and has been, almost totally ignored: "There is no escape for the conclusion that the sib [i.e., clan] evolved at least four times in North America and accordingly has had a multiple origin in the world. *Below I shall point out that there are several widespread conditions favoring the independent evolution of unilateral kinship*" (1920, p. 129; emphasis added).

A few years later Edward Sapir observed that "anthropology cannot long continue to ignore such stupendous facts as the independent development of sibs [clans] in different parts of the world. . . ." (1927, p. 104). I have no reference to statements such as the above from any other American anthropologist of that or subsequent periods.

If conditions conducive to the formation of clans were widespread, if clan organization had come into being independently in many areas of North America and of the world at large, why was it not assumed that if a tribe had clan organization it had developed it out of "conditions favoring the independent evolution of unilateral kinship" organization? Why did the assumption prevail that the presence of clan organization was an indication—if not proof—of diffusion?

One need not be an exceptionally perceptive reader of the history of ethnological theory to note that the obligation to be consistent rests rather lightly upon the logical shoulders of many ethnologists. Although Boas did say that clan organization "has arisen independently over and over again," his major emphasis in ethnology for many decades was upon the extensive and overriding influence of diffusion; a great part of his ethnographic work in the Northwest Coast of America was devoted to the reconstruction of culture history—who borrowed from whom (see White 1963, pp. 37 ff.). He was followed in this respect by virtually all of his major students, his students' students, and many others. Speaking for them, in a sense, Lowie was moved to declare that "the extensive occurrence of diffusion . . . encountered at every stage and in every phase of society, by itself lays the axe to the root of any [sic] theory of historical laws [i.e., evolutionism]" (1920, p. 424).

We shall review the history of the theory of diffusion of clan organization at some length for two reasons: (1) because it provides an excellent example of a problem that received only unsound explanation for decades but that is readily solved by the application of the concept of segmentation of cultural systems: and (2) because it provides a critique of the philosophy of ethnology taught to many generations of graduate students and accepted without question. It is high time that ethnologists review the work of their predecessors and give serious consideration to such things as (a) reflective thought, (b) what constitutes scientific evidence, and (c) the validity of the criteria by which conclusions are reached.

Boas' ethnographic studies of the Northwest Coast are replete with alleged instances of the diffusion of clans (White 1963). According to Lowie (1946, p. 229), "Boas found that in the interior of British Columbia clanless tribes with a family organization and a patrilineal trend adopted from coastal neighbors a matrilineal clan organization" (referring to Boas' paper, "Die Resultate der

Jesup-Expedition," presented at the XVI International Congress of Americanists in Vienna in 1909).

Lowie (1920, p. 434) tells us that "through diffusion the Southern Plains Indians come to share with the Iroquois . . . a type of sib [clan]." And, "clan systems have assuredly often been transmitted" (Lowie 1934, p. 145). Alexander Goldenweiser published an article on "The Diffusion of Clans in North America" (1918). He goes further than mere clan organization, however: "evidence abounds of the diffusion, in whole or in part, of social systems from tribe to tribe or from culture area to culture area" (Goldenweiser 1914, p. 436). Edward Sapir (1927, p. 103) asserts that "one is irresistibly led to believe that the social system arose only once in this area and that it was gradually assimilated by peoples to whom it was originally foreign. . . ." Clans, clubs, societies, etc. "spread . . . owing chiefly to imitation. . . ." Although Steward (1937, p. 91) deprecated "miracles of diffusion" to explain the presence of clans in neighboring tribes, he nevertheless asserts that "such institutions [i.e., clans, moieties, and other social forms] may obviously [*sic*] be introduced by diffusion." (1936, p. 334).

"Before leaving Boas' attitude toward diffusion," says Lowie (1937, p. 150), "we must note one other point. In contrast to those satisfied with establishing the *fact* of a historical connection, Boas regards this as merely an initial step. It is important to ascertain *why* traits were borrowed and *how* they were incorporated into the borrowing cultures" (Lowie's emphases).

But who, we may ask, has undertaken to tell us *why* and *how* clans have diffused? Boas acquired a great reputation for his "insistence on definite proof of cultural diffusion" (Lowie 1947, p. 304; see White 1966, pp. 12ff., for a review of the thesis that Boas' "unsparing mind exacted proof [*sic*] even in the complex and difficult situations

which prevail in culture . . ." Kroeber 1952, p. 146). Most
of the evidence used by Goldenweiser, Lowie, and other
disciples of Boas to support the assertion that clan organization diffuses readily from tribe to tribe came from
Boas' work in the Northwest Coast. Much of this "evidence" consisted of Boas' "it seems to my mind," or of information given him by the Kwakiutl Indians. "The processes [of diffusion] have been most carefully observed in the
Northwest coast area," says Goldenweiser; "the evidence
is conclusive" (Goldenweiser 1914, p. 419). Boas' asser-
tions were accepted as proof. As Radcliffe-Brown observed after coming to the United States: "I found many
students and anthropologists in America who had been so
throughly indoctrinated with the idea that the fact of the
diffusion of culture refutes any theory of social evolution
that it was impossible to discuss the subject. By some the
authority (or the supposed authority) of Boas in this matter was taken as final" (1931b, p. 81).

Boas cites many examples of diffusion of clan organization in his numerous papers on the Northwest Coast. Almost without exception the diffusion takes place as a consequence of "influence" exerted by a tribe having clans;
this "influence" appears to be exerted "at a distance,"
much as one heavenly body affects another through gravitational attraction. The "field student," Boas tells us (1924,
p. 341) "has ample evidence showing the ways in which
diffusion works." He cites "the introduction of the Badger
clan in Laguna by a Zuni woman" (ibid.). But Laguna already had clan organization. Had this pueblo been without clan organization, the Zuni woman could not have "introduced" the Badger clan; one clan in the midst of a
nonclan society would be meaningless.

What substantial evidence, if any, do we have of the diffusion of clan organization from a tribe possessing clans
to a clanless tribe? Dr. Elsie Clews Parsons (1936, p. 559)

reasoned "that Acoma [a Keresan pueblo in New Mexico] got its clan system from the Hopi is proved [*sic*] by the fact that the paternal aunt gives her godchild one of her clan's stock of personal names, a naming practice peculiar to the Hopi." This is the only instance of which I am aware where anyone has offered specific evidence of an alleged case of diffusion of clan organization. Actually, Dr. Parsons' argument proves nothing whatever. In the first place, she asserts that the naming practice in question was "peculiar to the Hopi." This is not substantiated; it is mere assertion, and the probability of such a "peculiarity" is very slight. Second, why not argue that it was the Hopi who obtained clan organization from Acoma? Third, if a clanless Acoma obtained clan organization from the Hopi, then we must assume that the other Keresan pueblos— Santo Domingo, San Felipe, Santa Ana, and Cochiti—obtained *their* respective clan systems from Acoma, all of which places a heavy burden upon Dr. Parsons' theory, to say the least.

Why would a clanless tribe "borrow" (i.e., obtain by way of diffusion) clan organization from a tribe possessing clans? Sapir (1927, p. 103) says that "it is owing chiefly to . . . imitation," which is just another way of saying that they obtained it; it does not tell us why they would "imitate." *How* would a clanless tribe go about borrowing clan organization from a neighbor? They would, first of all, have to discover and understand the way clan organization functioned in the tribe that had clans. Then they would have to work out lineages, genealogically, within their own tribe. Finally, they would have to decide the point at which they locate the ancestors from which the lineages had descended. This would be no easy matter. (In my field work among the Pueblos in New Mexico, I frequently traced a lineal grouping of kindred back to two women who had died a few generations previously. But my informants were unable to tell me whether they were "classificatory" sisters, or whether they had had the same biological mother.) Then, after the borrowing tribe had acquired clan organization, they would have had to articulate it with their political and ceremonial organizations. It is not easy to imagine any tribe undertaking all this— especially without an ascertainable motive.

We recall Boas' assertion that "we cannot deny its [i.e., diffusion's] existence in the development of *any* local cultural type [form]." We take this to mean that *any* cultural phenomenon may diffuse. But I do not accept this proposition. Items of material culture may diffuse readily. Folk tales are notorious for their propensity to spread from tribe to tribe and from region to region. Dances and rituals may diffuse. These traits, such as tools, ornaments, folk tales, rituals, etc., are discrete cultural elements that can pass freely from one tribe to another without loss to the tribe of origin or without requiring profound readjustment of the culture of the tribe that receives them. But clan organization is, and must be, an integral part of the social organization of the entire tribe; it is formed by the process of segmentation *within* the cultural system. A tribe could not "borrow" (i.e., obtain through diffusion) clan organization without fundamental reorganization of its entire social structure.

Without the concept of evolution the Boasian anthropologists could not see how clan organization emerges in an evolutionist process. Without the concept of cultural systems in general and the concept of segmentation in particular they could not understand how clans were formed. Their theory of the diffusion of clan organization was sheer assertion unsupported by either evidence or reason. They displayed no understanding of—or even concern with—the question of what constitutes scientific evidence. They consigned generations of students to unsound methods and conclusions. This is why I have thought it desirable to review this chapter in ethnological history in some detail in the hope of contributing to the refinement of our techniques of interpretation.

So far we have been dealing with organizations of cultural phenomena that are coterminous with the society, or cultural system, as a whole, such as custom, kinship organization, codes of ethics and etiquette, and segmented organization. We now turn to special structures within the cultural system, "organs" within the body politic. At this point we need not deal in detail with such special structures as headmen, shamans, nonhereditary chiefs, hereditary chiefs, councils of chiefs, etc. The reader is referred to discussion of these topics in *The Evolution of Culture* (1959b), chapter 8, "Integration, Regulation, and Control of Social Systems." These special structures, like systems such as ethics and etiquette, have been the work of cultural systems. As preliterate cultural systems evolve under the impetus of increased amounts of energy harnessed or advances in technology, these structures are produced in a series, from headman to council of chiefs. In civil societies, i.e., those produced by the Agricultural Revolution, the special mechanism by means of which the parts of the cultural system are coordinated, regulated, and controlled is the State-Church.

There are many similarities between biological organisms and cultural systems. The process of cultural evolution is marked by the same characteristics that are exhibited by the evolutionary process in the biological realm. These are not mere analogies. The cell and multicellular organism are made up of different kinds of parts that are organized into a unity regulated and controlled by the system as a whole. The same is true in the cultural realm. In the realm of biological organisms, the evolutionary process moves in a direction opposite to that specified for the cosmos as a whole by the Second Law of Thermodynamics, i.e., toward "negative entropy." The same is true of the evolution of culture. In the process of biological evolution we witness a progressive differentiation of structure and a corresponding specialization of function. The same is true in the cultural realm.

The structural features of civil societies are: (1) segments both geographic and social: provinces, principalities, wards, barrios, demes, states, etc.; (2) occupational classes such as guilds of craftsmen: metal workers, stone cutters, textile workers, etc., in addition to social classes such as sex, age, and marital status; (3) hierarchical classes, basically a dominant class and a subordinate class. The former exercises a virtual monopoly of power and of wealth; the latter are the servile classes: the serfs, slaves, peasants, wage-workers, etc. In civil society human rights and welfare are widely subordinated to property rights (see White 1959b, pp. 308–9, 329–30, 346–47). Thus, civil society is characterized by class division and conflict instead of mutual aid and cooperation that characterizes the cultures of preliterate cultural systems.

A cultural system so diversified structurally, with the potentialities and realities of conflict, both nonviolent in economic relations and violent as exhibited in the perennial uprisings of serfs, slaves, peasants, and proletariat throughout the entire history of civil society—such a cultural system must have a powerful (i.e., effective) mechanism to hold it together and prevent its destruction through insurrection and civil war. This mechanism is the State-Church, the former supplying physical force; the latter, doctrines of obedience and humility, coupled in some instances with the threat of dire punishment in the hereafter.

vectors of cultural systems

A CULTURAL system is composed of a variety of structures—organizations or groups—each having a magnitude and an objective. We call these structures "vectors," in analogy with the concept of vector in the field of physics or mathematics.* The agriculture industry is an example of a vector; so also are mining, manufacturing, etc. Organized labor, religious organizations, associations of physicians, bankers, schoolteachers, and scientists also are vectors. Various classes in society as a whole, such as minorities, women, and elderly, retired persons on a fixed or small income, are vectors. Even organized crime—if, indeed, this is a realistic concept—would constitute a vector.

Vectors may themselves be, and often are, composed of subvectors: the agriculture industry embraces animal husbandry, which is subdivided into horses, hogs, cattle (beef and dairy), and the cultivation of plants, subdivided into wheat, cotton, corn, truck gardening, etc. The ideological vector would consist of various philosophies: naturalism vs. supernaturalism; determinism vs. free will, etc.

Vectors have magnitude—force or power to influence other vectors and the cultural system as a whole. These magnitudes can be measured: the magnitude of the agricultural vector may be measured by number of farmers, acres of land cultivated, amount and value of commodities produced per man-year, etc. Its force or power is exhibited in its influence upon foreign trade, the cost of living, influence brought to bear upon legislatures, and

* Vector: a physical quantity with both magnitude and direction, such as a force or velocity (*Webster's New World Dictionary*).

administrative institutions. The magnitude of a religious organization is measured by the number of its members, the value of property it holds, the volume of its propaganda, etc. Its power is expressed in its ability to influence government on such matters as exemption from taxation, education of children, divorce, and abortion. The *objective* of the vector is, of course, to serve its own interests.

It is apparent that vectors are very real entities and are of the greatest importance in the structure and behavior of cultural systems. We shall encounter them later in this essay in the form of pressure groups and their lobbies.

the origin and growth of vectors and cultural systems

The first and most fundamental of cultural vectors was language. First, because culture, by definition, could not exist prior to articulate speech and language. Fundamental, because with the emergence of the ability to symbol, vocal utterances of prehuman primates were given a new dimension, namely, meaning freely and arbitrarily assigned. Freely, because there was no necessity to attach a particular meaning to a particular utterance. Arbitrarily, because any meaning could be assigned to any utterance: *kodo* could mean "nose," "go away," "acrid," or "yellow"; similarly, *nose* could be designated by any phonetic form (word). Thus, any word could mean anything and any meaning could be expressed by any word. The possibilities of correlation of meaning with vocal utterance were infinite.

No language could possibly make use of all available possibilities, or even a small fraction of them. Nor would a language that attempted to use a very large number of possibilities be practical and efficient. Languages arose in a process of social interaction; they had a very real function to perform—that of communicating information—information pertaining to emotions, attitudes, concepts, acts, and things. A premium was placed upon effectiveness, economy, and efficiency. The infinite number of possible correlations between meaning and utterance in a community of symboling primates had, therefore, to be drastically reduced to relatively few principles for any given language. Prefixes like *un-* or suffixes like *-ize* provide examples. Tenses could be expressed by verb endings (*hablo, hablaré*); number, by internal vocalic variation (mouse, mice). Meanings might be expressed by the tone of utterance.

In the Dakota language there was a large class of verbs, each having the prefix *ya-*, meaning that the action taken was done with the mouth in one way or another. Thus, *ya-ce-ya* (omitting the diacritical marks) meant "to make cry by talking or biting"; *ya-pin-za,* "to pull out hairs with the teeth"; *ya-ta-ku-ka,* "to make something of nothing in narrative."

In the language of the Nootka Indians, the structure of various things that were objects of transitive verbs was indicated by variations of the structure of the verb. Some languages were so constructed that "they crossed the river" could be expressed with a single word. Thus, the patterns and structures of a language like Chinese would be developed in one community—out of the range of infinite possibilities—a language like Athabascan or Greek would be developed in another.

Languages are not merely inert forms; they are dynamic systems. They grow and change. Grimm's Law expresses certain tendencies in Indo-European languages. Languages differentiate, become diversified into sublanguages and dialects. They compete with one another; some become archaic or extinct. They are an essential part of everything that people do *as human beings* (yawning, scratching, and sneezing do not involve symboling and therefore may not be considered *human* behavior). Language may inspire people to fight—even to the death—to decide which language shall be the official language of a province or city: Quebec, e.g., and instances of bloody riots in cities or provinces of India.

nude vs. non-nude art

Why has Western art, in sculpture and in painting, emphasized the nude human form whereas the art of China and Japan have not, but have focused upon things like mountains, water birds in a marsh, a clump of bamboo or a sprig of plum blossoms, temples, inns, or bridges—and people wearing clothes?

I cannot recall ever having heard an anthropologist (or any one else) ask this question. But we may be fairly sure of the kind of answer that this question would elicit: the answer would be psychological. One can imagine the field day that imaginative psychoanalysts would have with this query. Their answers would be derived by introspection rather than by observation of the real external world—cultural as well as noncultural. And, their answers would be plausible—to themselves and others to whom plausibility is accepted as verification. There is no evidence in biology or genetics to support a belief that the tendency toward nudity in art was inherent in the psyches of the ancient Greeks and the painters of Europe, whereas the psyches of the Japanese ran to carp and plum blossoms. Where, then, does the answer lie?

The answer is like the theory of the origin of languages. In depictive art as in language there was an almost infinite number of possibilities. One could choose—or hit upon—this or that subject and treat it in this or that way. But once a choice had been made (and if we could know what the particular circumstances were we could explain why one particular course was followed rather than another) it would develop along the path adopted and would tend to exclude other ways and forms: the original vector would inhibit the development of other and different vectors. Thus, we have the emergence of regional styles of art—in aboriginal Australia, among the Maya and the Aztecs, on the Northwest Coast of pre-Columbian America, in Egypt, Greece, and Western Europe.

This theory is applicable to musical styles also.

sin, salvation, and a redeemer

Judeo-Christian religion has been obsessed with the inherent sinfulness of the human race and salvation through a Redeemer. None of the other great religions—those of ancient Egypt, Greece and Rome, India and China, or aboriginal America—has these beliefs as the basic tenets of their theology. As a matter of fact, the sin-and-salvation complex seems aberrant in the galaxies of religion. Why is this so?

I believe the theory of vectors and systems provides the most fruitful approach to a reasonable answer. Somewhere along the line the religion of sin and salvation became established; later innovations could not compete successfully with the accepted modes and patterns and consequently did not develop.

If we knew as much about the social, economic, and political circumstances surrounding the origins of Christianity as we do of the origin of the "new religion" of the Iroquois—the Code of Handsome Lake—or of the Ghost Dance religion of Plains tribes of North America, we could make some progress in an attempt to answer the question here raised.

We find situations like this in other realms. If a kind of evergreen tree or if a grass establishes itself in a habitat, it tends to exclude other kinds of plant species. This occurs in regions that are capable of supporting a considerable variety of plant life. Thus we have evergreen forests and grassy plains. That natural habitats are often capable of supporting quite different kinds of plants and animals is made apparent by the Great Plains of North America that, after centuries of vast tracts of "buffalo grass" and millions of bison, came to nourish and sustain fields of wheat and corn and herds of dairy cow.

china vs. western europe: science and technology

Why have science and technology in the Eastern Hemisphere had their great development in the Occident rather than in the Orient? Specifically, why were the steam and internal combustion engines developed in Western Europe instead of in China?

In 150 B.C., a mathematical treatise in China dealt with problems of geometry and algebra as well as arithmetic. Chang Heng (ca. A.D. 78–139), a distinguished astronomer, determined the value of *pi* as the square root of 10. Heavenly bodies were systematically observed and records of the observations were kept; the first solar eclipse was recorded in 775 B.C.; a comet was noted in 613 B.C.

Technologically, China was more advanced than Western Europe prior to A.D. 1500. Diffusion of inventions and even migrations of craftsmen were from the East to the West, rather than from the West to the East. Here is a partial list of certain techniques that diffused from China to the West (Singer 1956, pp. 770–71):

> Gunpowder; mariner's compass; fore-and-aft rigged ships; paper, printing with movable type; cable suspension bridges; canals with lock-gates; triphammer mill with water power; rotary winnowing-machine with crank-handle; blowing-engines for furnaces and forges with waterpower; piston-bellows for continuous blast;

silk and silk-working machines; wheelbarrow; the box kite (the ancestor of heavier-than-air craft); deep drilling for water, brine, and natural gas; iron casting; efficient draught-harness for horses (with breast-strap and collar); seed-drill plough with hopper; porcelain.

Why then did not China combine science and technology and surpass, or equal, the West after A.D. 1500 as it did in the millenium prior to this time?

Vectoral analysis is pertinent here also. This analysis, and a fairly full record of cultural historical events, would unquestionably illuminate this whole problem and enable us to achieve a substantial answer to our question.

Philosophic inquiry and concern may turn to the external world or it may turn inward to the self. While Europe was "developing a technique for knowing and controlling matter," says Yu-Lan Fung in his essay "Why China Has No Science," China was developing a technique "for knowing and controlling the mind" (p. 258). The Chinese philosophers "had no need of scientific certainty, because it was themselves that they wished to know; so in the same way they had no need of the power of science, because it was themselves that they wished to conquer" (p. 261).

In Western Europe the vector of Christian theology competed with the growing vector of rational scientific thought. In China the philosophic vector concerned with self reduced to naught the vector concerned with knowing and controlling the external world.

In China a marked change of cultural orientation took place during the Han Dynasty (202 B.C.–A.D. 220), according to Turner. There was a resurgence of supernaturalism and traditionalism, a "reorientation of Confucianism, the elaboration of Taoism, and the acceptance of Buddhism, [which] disintegrated the secular outlook and rational methodology which, although they were never clearly developed in the philosophies, might have produced a science if social and economic conditions had strengthened them. . . . eventually science became identified with the Chinese low intellectual tradition, while the Chinese high intellectual tradition developed mainly as a body of ritualistic and decorative learning" (Turner 1941, pp. 848–49).

The Chinese political system, with its competitive examinations based upon the Classics as the basis for holding office, and its emphasis upon Confucianism, ethics, and the self, provided neither the soil nor the climate for scientific and technological advance.

The foregoing is far from an adequate explanation of the different courses followed by China and Western Europe. *Why* did Chinese culture concern itself with the mind rather than with the external world? *Why* was there a marked resurgence of supernaturalism and traditionalism during the Han dynasty? I believe that both Yu-lan Fung and Ralph Turner are dealing with vectors. This problem is presented as an invitation to other scholars who would like to test the fruitfulness of the method of vector analysis.

vectors "have a life of their own"

A body at rest remains at rest; a body in motion will continue in motion, in a straight line and forever, unless its course and its motion are influenced by an outside force. The tendency of customs, institutions, tools, and techniques to persist, beyond the boundaries of efficiency and sometimes even of usefulness, is notorious; we usually call this "conservatism," as if this explained the phenomenon. A custom exists; so does a pebble on a mountainside. The custom persists, i.e., continues to exist; so does the stone on the mountainside. Existence has a time dimension (continuity) as well as a spatial dimension; being is also doing.

Culture and cultural vectors grow by themselves. As we have noted earlier, culture is a process *sui generis,* a stream in which cultural things and events produce other cultural things and events, just as meteorological events bring about other meteorological events. Concepts interact, form new syntheses: Copernican, Keplerean, Galilean concepts are synthesized in the nervous system of a Newton, forming the laws of gravitation. "The theory of Clerk Maxwell and Lorentz led inevitably to the theory of relativity," says Einstein (1934, p. 57). The experiments of Faraday and the mathematical formulations of Clerk Maxwell led to the invention of apparatus to produce electromagnetic waves and to Marconi's invention of the radio (from "How to Become a Mathematician" by Bertrand Russell, Haldeman-Julius booklet). Tools beget tools: "every tool has a genealogy . . . it is descended from the tools by which it has itself been constructed. The clockmakers' lathes of the eighteenth century have led through a clear historical chain of intermediate tools to the great turret lathes of the present day" (Wiener 1950, p. 167).

Language is a self-reproducing vector, a process *sui generis.* It is a stream of sounds, of articulate vocal utterances, which flows through a particular species of primate: Man. It enters the biological system of the infant and is eventually passed on to others; it flows from one being to another and from one generation to another. Language is the stimulus; articulate speech is the response. Language provides the medium of human social intercourse and the means of contact with, and the interpretation of, the external world. If it is Homo sapiens that carries language within itself, it is language that recreates humanity in its manifold features with every new-born child; it transforms mere primates into human be-ings. The flow of language can no more stop than can the biological process of reproduction that makes its continuity possible; it must go on while and as we live. We are powerless to stop it; we are helpless in its grasp.

Much the same observation can be made with regard to other vectors: the use of chopsticks, smoking, baseball, etc., but with this difference: Language is a vector that has no competitors; it is that or nothing. But the use of chopsticks, rickshaws, automobiles, baseball games, and grand opera are vectors that compete with other vectors in the cultural system and are therefore influenced and modified—or even extinguished—by them. "We" cannot "stop using" chopsticks, baseball games, or comic strips, but these arts may be discontinued in the competitive process with other vectors.

supersonic transport (SST)

In the biological realm orthogenetic lines of evolution have achieved maxima in size, weight, and speed of living creatures—dinosaurs, whales, mammoths, cheetahs, hawks. In the cultural realm also, the orthogenetic process has produced maxima in various forms: pyramids, temples, obelisks, colosseums in the ancient world; sky-scrapers, gigantic dams, bridges, oceangoing ships, and great aircraft. In the latter category we witness vectors enlarging themselves, or increasing their speeds, primarily to realize the possibilities within themselves only, e.g., speed for speed's sake. Hence: the SST. The process of development has not been a rational one, i.e., in the sense of responding to a rational need and of serving this need in a rational way in cost and product. The heavier-than-aircraft vector, which began with the box kite in ancient China, evolved through several stages and in a rational way as we have defined this term above. The evolution of aircraft became self-contained, a process orthogenetic, *sui generis*. Faster planes were built because faster planes could be built (the mountain climber climbs because the mountain is there).

The plane itself is but the heart and core of a huge socioeconomic and technological complex: laboratories and factories, engineers and skilled workmen, large corporations with executives, stockholders, and dividends. The federal government has subsidized the project with vast sums of money—in the face of desperate need for mass transit systems in great metropolitan areas.

What will the SST accomplish? It will enable people to fly from New York to London or Rome in two hours, plus or minus, less than they could by conventional jets. But saving time would be offset by fewer passengers carried. The cost of flight would prevent all but the super-rich and the subsidized from using the SST. Some countries have declared that they would not permit the SST to land at conventional airports or near metropolitan areas. The time and distance from landing field and urban destination of passengers might offset the time gained in flight. It is said that the noise of takeoff and landing would be unbearable to residents anywhere near the airport. In flight, the SST would pour tons of pollutants into the atmosphere, contributing to the uninhabitability of the planet.

But, as we have noted, it is not just the swift airplane to be considered. There are the laboratories, factories, executives, stockholders, employees—and politicians who want "to make jobs" for workers—and their votes. And those who are possessed by the delusion of Manifest Destiny.

competition and conflict of cultural vectors

Each vector asserts itself by its very existence; it has an impact upon other vectors and exerts an influence upon

the cultural system as a whole. These vectors may compete with one another much as species—foxes, rabbits,
eagles—compete with one another within the territory
they occupy. Out of these processes of adaptation and
competition comes the so-called balance of nature. In relatively stable cultural systems there is a situation of "live
and let live" among cultural vectors. But many cultural
systems are not stable; radical innovations, such as the
origin of horticulture, metallurgy, and the advent of steam
power, upset their balance. Competition may become
more intense; some vectors may be extinguished: metal
tools replace stone tools; factories extinguish handicraft
production; the automobile renders the horse and buggy
extinct.

The career of the automobile is a case in point. Its immediate target of competition was the horse-and-buggy,
but its impact was rapidly extended to the entire horse-
as-a-prime-mover complex: harness makers, carriage
makers, producers of hay and feed grains, blacksmiths who
shod the horses, the livery stable business, street sweep-
ers, etc. But the competition did not stop here: the automobile eventually extinguished almost all railroad passenger traffic—not merely transcontinental and interstate,
but interurban and metropolitan traffic as well. This has
taken place, not because automobile travel is quicker,
more efficient, and cheaper. It has taken place because
the automotive vector in our cultural system has grown in
magnitude and power in its constituent parts and forces,
creating huge automobile factories with hundreds of
thousands of employees and stockholders. The industry is
fertilized by millions of dollars of advertising; the highway
lobby and the federal government have provided the high-
ways and the expressways. A shiny, new automobile is a
beautiful thing; it is, in many instances, the most beauti-

ful, precious thing in the lives of millions upon millions of Americans.

As a result of this acromegalic growth, the automobile has become a tumor in the body politic. With x million automobiles carrying $1.2 x$ million people to work in metropolitan centers, congestion, often with bumper-to-bumper traffic, results—this and a lethal pall of noxious gases hovering above the metropolis.* A rational mass transit system would increase the speed and comfort of the men and women going to work, do it more cheaply, and reduce the pollution of the atmosphere to less than bearable proportions. In a loyal attempt to defend the automobile, a citizen expostulated: "Yes, but the automobile is the only way we have to get there." This is just the point: the automobile has all but extinguished other means of transportation in many areas of society; we are at its mercy. In accord with a maxim of our culture—not made explicit but obvitus and valid inferentially—"Don't do anything until the crisis threatens to overwhelm you," our cultural system is wrestling with the question of mass transit systems in metropolitan areas and rapid transit between cities.

An excellent example of conflict of vectors and the value of the concept of vector as an explanatory device is provided by the contest between Christian theology and science in Western Europe between the Middle Ages and the twentieth century. The history of the rivalry of these two intellectual traditions is well told in A. D. White's scholarly *History of the Warfare of Science with Theology in Christendom* (1896). We shall deal only with the fundamental point at issue—divine creation vs. natural evolution.

---

* "The automobile will choke our society to death," Leonard Woodcock, president of the United Auto Workers, as quoted by UPI, *Santa Barbara News Press,* March 16, 1972, p. A–10.

I must preface this account with a report on my experience in teaching a course in the history of anthropology for many years. To many students the situation was simple: the theory of divine creation was contradicted by the discovery of human remains in association with fossils of extinct animals. Therefore, theology was abandoned and science was accepted in its place. And, it was assumed, though not asserted, that it was Darwin's *On the Origin of Species* that dealt the blow, so to speak. But the series of events require a very different interpretation. One discovery of the contiguity of human and extinct animals would have been sufficient to refute the theory of divine creation. But it took repeated discovery of such associations over a period of centuries to elevate and securely establish the theory of evolution. Moreover, the theory of divine creation was *not* extinguished—as it would have been had the contest been one of logic and evidence as my students (along with millions of others) assumed.

The contest was not between "right and wrong" as established by fossils and strata. The contest was between two vectors, between two intellectual traditions, each of which had a magnitude, a weight, an influence. The problem was *culturological* rather than *logical*. The question was not which was correct and which was incorrect. The question was, which vector was the stronger—stronger in the sense of exerting influence within a cultural system? Unless one can think in terms of vectors and their magnitudes and influence he cannot comprehend the *History of the Warfare of Science with Theology* and *On the Origin of Species.*

It will be recalled that Archbishop James Usher (1581–1656) determined the date at which the Creation took place: 4004 B.C. Dr. John Lightfoot (1828–1889), Hulsean professor of divinity at Cambridge, was more precise: "Heaven and earth, entire and circumference, were created together, in the same instant, and clouds full of water. . . . and man was created by the Trinity on the 23rd of October, 4004 B.C., at 9 o'clock in the morning" (Greenwich time, presumably).

Stone implements that came to light from time to time were called "thunder stones." One theory was that they fell from the heavens during the expulsion of Lucifer. Large fossilized bones were the remains of animals destroyed in the Flood. Or, they were evidence that "there were giants in the earth on those days."

During the closing years of the sixteenth century Michele Mercati (1541–1593) argued that flint arrowheads were man-made. He called attention to the use of flint knives among the Jews, and to stone tools and weapons used by the American Indians. He believed that the early inhabitants of Italy also used stone tools for similar purposes (Hodgen 1964, p. 157, n.34). It is significant to note that Mercati was the keeper of the botanical garden of Pope Pius V and that he was the founder of the Vatican Museum. His book was not published until the seventeenth century.

In *Preadamitae,* published in Amsterdam in 1655, Isaac de la Peyrère tried to prove that Adam and Eve were not the first human beings upon the earth. His book was publicly burned and La Peyrère was thrown into prison and forced to recant.

These skeptics were, of course, only a few among many who questioned the dogmas of Christian theology. So much for theory, now to turn to hard-fact evidence.

In 1715 a flint point was found in a gravel bed in association with the bones of an elephant in London. The specimens and a record of the find were preserved. In 1723, Antoine de Jussieu addressed the French Academy on the Origin and Uses of Thunder-stones, showing that travelers from various parts of the world had brought weapons and tools of stone to France that were essentially similar to the so-called thunder-stones of Europe. A year later Father J. F. Lafitau, who had been a missionary among North American Indians, published *Moeurs des sauvages americans comparée aux moeurs des premiers temps* (Paris, 1724). He regarded primitive peoples as exemplifying stages in the development of culture.

In 1771 Johann Friedrich Esper found human bones in association with the remains of cave bear and other extinct animals in the German Jura mountains. John Frere discovered Acheulean handaxes associated with the remains of extinct animals in Suffolk in 1790. He published an account of his find in 1800, but his discovery went virtually unnoticed. In 1823 Ami Boué, of the Vienna Academy of Sciences, claimed to have found human fossil remains associated with remains of extinct animals in quaternary deposits in Austria. Also in 1823, William Buckland, the first Reader in Geology at Oxford, later dean of Westminster, discovered the "Red Lady of Paviland"—actually, the skeleton of a young man—associated with Paleolithic implements in a cave in Wales. Between 1825 and 1829 Father J. MacEnery excavated in Kent's Cavern where he found flint implements in association with the remains of such extinct animals as the rhinoceros, under the stratified unbroken floor of stalagmite of the cavern. "These remains seemed to MacEnery to demonstrate beyond doubt the coexistence of man and extinct animals at a very remote time in the past—certainly before 4004 B.C.—but his views were not shared by many of those with whom he discussed his excavations" (Daniel 1950, p. 35).

M. Tournal (in 1828) and Christol (in 1829), excavating in the south of France, found human remains alongside those of the extinct hyena and rhinoceros. Dr. P. C. Schmerling began excavation of caves in Belgium about 1833. He too found human remains along with those of skeletons of rhinoceros and mammoth. Charles Lyell visited Schmerling and published a vivid description of, and tribute to, Dr. Schmerling's indefatigable labors in *The Antiquity of Man,* 1863.

In 1840 Godwin Austin presented to the Royal Geological Society an account of his discoveries in Kent's Cavern, setting forth a description of human remains mingled with those of cave bear, hyena, rhinoceros, and other extinct animals. Because of prevailing indifference and skepticism, however, his paper was not published.

The review that I have just presented does not include, by any means, all those who undertook similar investigations and provided the same kind of evidence of the antiquity of man. And I shall not continue the review beyond the time and work of Boucher de Perthes. My purpose is not to present even a brief historical review of the facts, but rather to inquire into the significance of the facts.

A single discovery of human remains associated with those of extinct animals would have been sufficient to decide the question at issue—divine creation c. 4004 B.C. or a tremendously long process of evolution. Why, then, did it take a few centuries before the theory of evolution could become widely accepted? *

The answer to this question is that the question was *not* a merely logical one: if *a* is true, then *b* is not true (*is* there a luminiferous ether between sun and earth that makes possible the transmission of light and heat or is there not such an ether?). It was a question of the relative magnitudes of cultural vectors. It was not a matter of mere choice of concepts. The traditions involved were not merely conceptual; they were sociological, economic, po-

---

* Dr. Harlow Shapley, an eminent Harvard astronomer, tells us that "in its early days Harvard College stood by the geocentric interpretation [of the solar system] for more than a century after the apperance of *De Revolutionibus Orbium Coelestium* by Copernicus, 1543" (1967, p. 37).

litical—in short, *cultural* traditions. Social, ecclesiastical, economic (property rights), political institutions were involved; they were not to be destroyed because of an error in arithmetic (or chronology). The vector of Christianity had centuries behind it. It was an integral part of an ecclesiastical-political organization that had great authority and power. Belief in the Creation was widespread and deep-seated. Beliefs that challenged the authority of the Church could be branded as heresy and severely punished. Galileo, Buffon, and many others were forced to recant their beliefs that rested upon both evidence and reason. The first edition of *Encyclopaedia Britannica* (1768–1771), contained articles on "creation," (made possible only by God's power), a detailed description of Noah's Ark, etc. The *Britannica* of 1810 contained an article on "Antediluveans" that validated the Holy Scriptures.

Opposition to naturalism and science did not come from religious sources only, however. Cuvier (1769–1832) was unquestionably one of the most eminent men of science of his time. He has been regarded as the founder of the sciences of comparative anatomy and paleontology. He was a professor at the College de France and chancellor of the University of Paris. As inspector of education and the head of a committee on education, he exerted great influence upon higher education in France. He became a baron in 1819 and a peer in 1831. He was the embodiment of "the Establishment." His prestige was great; his influence enormous. He threw the weight of his influence and authority on the side of theology and against science. Specifically, and as an example, he opposed the conclusions reached by Boué. Cuvier accounted for the remains of extinct animals, which had been found repeatedly, by the theory of a series of catastrophes that destroyed all life, followed by repeated creations.

In the competition between Christian theology and science we observe a mature intellectual tradition, firmly entrenched in the institutions of both church and state, being challenged by a naturalistic tradition that had a number of beginnings and that grew slowly bit by bit, until it was large enough and strong enough to successfully challenge the religious tradition,* and a freedom to express itself equally with the religious vector.

The theory of vectors is adaptable and illuminating to a specific case: the publication of *On the Origin of Species* (1859). It was an epoch-making book; Sir James Jeans speaks of "the Darwinian revolution." Why is this book regarded as a great landmark in the history of science and of folk thought in general? The theories of Darwin were anticipated by many thinkers and men of science: his grandfather Erasmus Darwin, Buffon, J. C. Prichard, Lamarck, Quatrefages—who wrote a book, *Darwin et ses precurseurs français*—and others. (See also Thomson n.d.) There was nothing new in *The Origin of the Species,* with the possible exception of the theory of natural selection; that, however, was crystallized in Darwin's mind by a reading of Thomas Robert Malthus' *An Essay on the Principle of Population* (1789). Why, then, was *On the Origin of Species* such a great book? The theory of vectors in an evolutionary process helps us answer this question. The publication of *On the Origin of Species* happened to be *the weight that tipped the scales between the competing vectors of science and theology in the favor of science;* it broke the back of theological opposition.

It is significant to note that the theological vector—even

---

* "The essential point is that, when there are only a few fossils, the climate of opinion may be more important than the fossils in determining how they are regarded. . . . it takes repeated discoveries to change the patterns of thought that took form in the period when fossils were few" (Washburn 1968, p. 102).

in orthodox form and content—did not wither and die
after the existence of man a million years before 4004 B.C.
had been demonstrated and his evolutionary development
from anthropoid forms documented by an abundance of
paleontological evidence, as would have been the case if
the issue had been merely one of logic—a choice between
"true" and "not true." Western culture (like other great
cultures) has many traditions. They might be thought of as
great pieces of a cultural pie. They are social, economic,
and political organizations as well as intellectual traditions—as Durkheim tried to teach us many years ago.
They cannot be exorcized by logic nor annihilated by
legislative enactment. They may be logically (rationally) in-
compatible with one another and still be viable in a functioning system. Thus, a person may be a good biologist
and believe in the Virgin Birth. A great nation may be of-
ficially atheistic while its churches are full at Eastertime.
Few things could be more devastating to a modern, com-
plexly structured cultural system than the strict imposition
of the principles of logical rationality upon it.

lobbying

A CULTURAL system, such as a modern nation, is composed of many and varied interests. Each strives to achieve security and to enlarge its advantage. In 1787, James Madison wrote the following in No. 10 of the *Federalist Papers:*

"A landed interest, a manufacturing interest, a mercantile interest, a monied interest, and many lesser interests, grow up of necessity in civilised nations, and divide them into different classes, actuated by different sentiments and views. The regulation of these various and interfering interests forms the principal task of modern legislation, and involves the spirit of party and faction in the necessary and ordinary operations of the government (*The Federalist,* p. 43).

This pithy comment on "interests" contains the germ of modern lobbyists and lobbying.

An intimate relationship between "interests" and government is natural and inevitable. But government in a democratic-capitalist cultural system such as the United States does not possess special mechanisms to deal with these interests directly. Government is organized upon a territorial, or areal, basis: states, congressional districts, counties, cities, wards, etc. Whose interest does a congressman, elected by a congressional district, serve—the farmer, the manufacturer, banker, landlord, wage laborer, or shopkeeper? The major parties are dedicated to serving all the people, in theory at least; they make no provision for specific interests.

Therefore, they must shift for themselves. "It is characteristic of interests," says Milbrath (1963, p. 199), "that they seek representation in governmental decision-making; if they cannot find adequate representation through formal governmental or semi-governmental channels, they will seek other channels." "Furthermore," he observes elsewhere (1968, p. 443), "American parties cannot be counted on for firm policy leadership. Interest groups in the United States have almost abandoned working through parties and instead have hired lobbyists to secure policy representation." Hence, lobby groups and lobbyists have "evolved as a part of government to fulfill this need for specific representation, a need that no other component of the political process is adapted to fill" (ibid., p. 445). Lobby groups have been called "an invisible arm of government"; "the third house of Congress," etc.

The competition and conflict of vectors in a national cultural system is, therefore, carried on in the arena in which the interests cited by Madison—and many others—meet and contest with one another. The competition is vigorous and often ruthless; governmental regulation usually leaves room, through exceptions and loopholes, for considerable freedom for the interest and its representative. On the face of it, the competitive struggle does not appear to be one of *this* vector versus *that* vector or vectors: the dairy vector versus the tobacco interests or those of veteran groups. Each vector strives to have its own interest served, regardless of the welfare of other vectors or of the society as a whole; "it's everyone for himself and let the devil take the hindmost."

The term "lobbyist" is used rather loosely; it has at least three meanings: (1) it is used interchangeably with "pressure group," any organization or person that endeavors to influence the decisions of government; (2) any person who, on behalf of some other person or group and usually for pay, attempts to influence legislation through direct contact with legislators; and (3) anyone who is required to register or report his spending under the terms of the Federal Regulation of Lobbying Act of 1946 (*Congressional Quarterly Service* [*CQS*] 1968, p. 4). Lobbying occurs on all levels of government in the United States: city and county as well as national. Also, lobbying occurs as readily with executive branch officials as with legislatures.

The Washington telephone directory lists some 1,200 trade, business, and professional associations (Deakin 1966, p. 123). Pendleton Herring (1967) presents a list of organizations represented in Washington; it is almost seven pages long, two columns per page. It would be rather difficult to find any grouping large enough to be considered an "interest" that does not have a representative in Washington to promote its interests. It is difficult, also, to classify these organizations. We can specify a few of the larger and more powerful classes, however.

There are the giant corporations such as Standard Oil of New Jersey, General Motors, and A.T. & T. There are associations of interests such as the American Bankers Association and the National Association of Electric Companies. Agriculture and dairying are represented by the Farm Bureau Federation, the National Milk Producers Federation, and others. The AFL-CIO, the National Federation of Post Office Clerks, and other interest groups comprise the labor interest. There are racial groups, church groups, civil rights groups, reform organizations, veterans' associations, thirty womens' interest groups; the big business groups of the National Association of Manufacturers and the Chamber of Commerce of the United States; education and science are represented, and so on ad infinitum.

A number of states and some cities maintain offices in Washington to represent their interests. The same is true for some foreign countries.

Lobbying, like everything else in today's culture, has its history. During the era of the second half of the nineteenth century, big business barons were represented in

Congress by senators; according to William Allen White (as quoted by Deakin 1966, p. 107) "one Senator represented the Union Pacific Railway System, another the New York Central, still another the insurance interests . . . cotton had half a dozen senators. . . . And so it went." James Bryce obtained a sorry picture of lobbying from "an experienced American publicist," who described it as "so disagreeable and humiliating that all men shrink from it" (Bryce 1910, 1: 694). "Dinners, receptions, and other entertainments, by the arts of social life and the charms of feminine attraction" were employed in the art of lobbying. "Women were at one time among the most active and successful lobbyists in Washington," Bryce reports, adding that "very few are now seen" (ibid., 695). Bryce also speaks of "the professional staff of lobbyists in Washington" (ibid., 694).

Writing in 1968, Milbrath states that there were "between eight hundred and one thousand registered lobbyists in Washington" (p. 443). Some lobbyists work on a part-time basis, but many, if not most of them, are on a full-time, professional basis. Journalist Deakin speaks of lobbying as "big business," "a major industry" (1966, p. 105). He cites the National Association of Electric Companies as an example: it reported spending $547,000 in lobbying in one year.

Lobbyists come from a variety of walks of life. Some are persons who are intimately acquainted with Washington and the mode of life of the men and women in government. Many are attorneys; many big corporations retain law firms to represent their interests. Many ex-congressmen, both senators and representatives, have become lobbyists. The *CQS* (1968) presents a five-page review of former congressmen who have served as lobbyists: Senators Scott W. Lucas, James P. Kem, and Prentiss M. Brown being notable examples. In the House, Harold O.

Lovre and Albert L. Reeves, Jr., had impressive records as lobbyists. Aides to the president and members of the cabinet have also engaged in lobbying.

Between 1949 and 1965 two vigorous battles were fought over the issue of medical care, which illustrates the way lobbying is carried on—illustrates the way that various vectors of the cultural system cooperate and compete with one another—until a decision is reached. The first battle was fought over President Truman's proposal for a compulsory national health insurance program (1949). Favoring the proposal were the AFL-CIO, Americans for Democratic Action, American Association of Social Workers, the National Farmers Union, and other organizations. Opposed were the Chamber of Commerce of the United States, the American Legion, American Farm Bureau Federation, General Federation of Womens' Clubs, the Committee for Constitutional Government, Blue Cross-Blue Shield Commissions, American Pharmaceutical Association and other groups. But, leading the opposition was the American Medical Association (AMA).

The AMA launched a large scale publicity campaign, employing a public relations firm for this purpose, warning the citizens of the United States against "socialized medicine." This campaign cost the AMA $1.5 million in 1949 and $1.3 million in 1950, according to reports filed with the Clerk of the House as required by the Lobbying Act of 1946. Again in 1965, the AMA led the fight against a program for national medical care. "It unleashed two major nationwide publicity campaigns in newspapers, radio and television . . . at a cost of $1.2 million . . . the third highest amount ever recorded for lobbying spending, exceeded only by the AMA's spending in 1949–50" (*CQS*, 1968, pp. 78–79).

During the 1960s the United States had under consideration the installation of a "thin" antiballistic missile (ABM) system to protect the nation against possible missile attack by Communist China. Secretary of Defense Robert S. McNamara opposed the system as "too expensive, unreliable, and inferior in deterrent value to a strong U.S. offensive missile force." But by 1967, more than $2.4 billion had been spent on research for the system by various powerful companies with defense contracts. It was estimated that more than 15,000 companies stood to profit from the installation of the system—powerful corporations such as General Electric, Sperry-Rand, General Dynamics, McDonnell-Douglas, and many others. *The New Republic* (March 11, 1967) estimated that "28 of the major contractors for the ABM project employed about one million persons in 172 Congressional districts in 42 states" (CQS, 1968, p. 57). The pressures of these interest groups upon the Congress were overwhelming, and the Secretary of Defense was obliged to capitulate to the "military-industrial complex."

The *CQS* presented a list of 38 corporations each of which had been awarded prime military contracts totaling more than $1 billion during the years 1961 to 1967, inclusive. Seven of these corporations—25 percent—were awarded contracts in excess of $5 billion. Lockheed Aircraft led with a total of $10.6 million.

gun control legislation

According to the *CQS* (1968, p. 85), "there were 6,400 murders, 10,000 suicides and 2,600 accidental deaths caused by firearms in 1966. In Japan, where no one except police officers is permitted to own a pistol, there were only 37 firearm murders in 1962. By contrast, in the United States, which has about twice the population of Japan, there were 5,954 homicides by firearms that year." The Louis Harris survey of 1968 reported that 51 percent of American households possessed guns. But 70 percent of the people interviewed favored the passage of federal laws to place tight controls over the sale of guns. "Of the people who owned guns, 65 percent favored firearms control" (p. 85). Demand for more control over the sale and possession of handguns, especially, has become greater, due in part at least, to the series of assassinations that have punctuated political and social issues in recent years.

There are a number of associations that are opposed to gun control legislation: the National Shooting Sports Foundation, the Sporting Arms and Ammunition Manufacturers' Institute, wildlife and conservation organizations, etc. Many manufacturers of firearms have offices in Washington, such as Colt, Du Pont (parent company of Remington), Olin Mathieson (Winchester-Western), etc. But the National Rifle Association (NRA) is, according to *CQS,* "by far the most powerful pressure group against strong firearms-control measures" (p. 86). But the NRA has never registered as a lobbying group, and only a few of the manufacturers have registered lobbyists, apparently.

After the assassination of President Kennedy with a mail-order carbine equipped with a telescopic sight, *The American Rifleman* magazine, published by the NRA, "expressed shock over the 'incredible tragedy' and then condemned the 'wave of antifirearm feeling and almost universal demand for tighter controls over the mail-order sales of guns,' much of which the magazine said was 'hysterical in nature' " (*CQS,* 1968, p. 85).

There has been much, and often bitter, controversy over the issue of gun control legislation. *CQS* summarizes the position of each side, presents the pros and the cons, and gives the names of senators (among whom was Robert F. Kennedy) and representatives on each side. To some it seems that the demand for more or tighter legislative controls is growing with each new assassination, accomplished or attempted, but so far the opponents of such legislation have been able to hold their ground.

The discussion of lobbyists makes our presentation of the theory of vectors of cultural systems concrete, vivid, and convincing. The competitive struggle of interests, spearheaded by their respective lobbyists, carried on by personal contact with legislators and members of the executive department, by letters-to-your-congressmen campaigns, campaigns managed by professional public relations firms, etc., presents in graphic terms the behavior of cultural systems. Out of the competition of interests emerges a synthesis and action on the basis of this synthesis, whether it means retaining the status quo or effecting change.

are lobbies good or bad?

"Are lobbies good or bad?" is a question that many students of the subject ask themselves, usually at the conclusion of their studies. In the past, lobbying has been coarse, crude, and corrupt. Government has attempted to reform this inevitable process in a free enterprise system, to minimize corruption, and to raise ethical standards. The Congress and the courts have apparently tried to serve both sides: they have provided enough restrictive legislation to appease those who want governmental regulation and control, and at the same time they have permitted great freedom for the lobbyists. The legislation and court decisions have left the situation full of ambiguities, exceptions to rules, and loopholes for evasion (Milbrath 1963, part 4). In the language of vector theory, a balance has been struck between the vector of regulation and control and the vector of "free enterprise," a contest that has characterized the entire system of the United States for many decades.

It appears to be easier to support the proposition that lobbies are "bad" than to present a substantial and convincing brief that they are "good." This is probably due, in large part at least, to the fact that most lobbies are trying to promote a special interest without regard to the welfare of society. Even the lobbies that state they have only the general welfare at heart are not without opposition. The very existence of a lobby is a de facto admission that it is exerting itself against opposition: there is no lobby encouraging citizens to eat, but there have been and still are lobbies to persuade them to eat or drink some particular thing, or prevent them from doing so (butter vs. margarine, e.g.).

Our authorities try hard, apparently to find something favorable to say about lobbies. Milbrath (1968, p. 445) is an example: "perhaps the most useful service [of lobbies] is the transmission of viewpoints. This serves a creative function in alerting decision makers to all possible alternatives"—faint praise.

Journalist Deakin begins *The Lobbyists* (1966) with this comment:

> As this book goes to press, lobbyists for special interest groups continue their unceasing battle against new proposals to advance the general welfare, to restore the nation's cities as decent places to live, to expand educational and economic opportunities for the underprivileged and to allocate America's material bounty more equitably. Lobbyists are working hard to prevent regulation of the interstate traffic in firearms and to block legislation protecting the consumer from hidden credit charges and misleading packaging. . . . (p. vi)

But Deakin, too, can find something nice to say about lobbying: "Lobbying is an integral and often constructive part of the legislative process, both as a source of information that Congress must have in the enactment of sound laws and as an outlet for the aims and desires of special interests" (ibid.).

It is not my prerogative, much less my duty, to pass moral judgment upon lobbying. Cultural systems are not ethical or moral systems, as I have previously pointed out. They behave in terms of their intrinsic properties in accordance with the principle of cause and effect. Are foxes who eat pheasants "bad"? Are comets with parabolic orbits "good"? Is it "bad" for a corporation to grow to great size, eliminating weaker corporations along the way? Is it "bad" for a nation, a cultural system, to do what its most powerful segments want to do?

We leave such questions to the moralists who, incidentally, will be distributed among many camps. Our job is simple: it is to explain, to make intelligible, the behavior of cultural systems.

cultural systems as entities

CULTURAL systems are in actuality as well as by definition unities, integers. We remind the reader of this fact after a lengthy discussion of the behavior and relative autonomy of vectors. We are not faced here with a question of priority: Which comes first, the vector or the system? They come into being and exist simultaneously. Our attention may focus now upon the one, now upon the other. We now wish to focus upon the whole.

In considering the parts of which a cultural system is composed we distinguish between the mere number of parts, or the number of like parts, and the number of different kinds of parts. At the bottom of the evolutionary scale of cultural systems we find highly undifferentiated structures, i.e., systems with a small number of like parts and a minimum number of unlike parts. The horde of the aborigines of Australia will serve as an example. It is defined principally by the locality in which the people live and find their subsistence. It is composed of families (segments) and classes—male, female, married, single, adult, child, aged, etc. Division of labor is limited to the division of society into two classes: men and women. There is no specialization along occupational lines and there are virtually no special group structures, such as recognized headmen and chiefs. As a matter of fact, the horde is very similar structurally to the societies of some anthropoid or simian societies.

As we go up the scale of cultural evolution we encounter different kinds of components of cultural systems: lineages, moieties, clans, and also special structures, i.e., mechanisms of integration, regulation, and control, such as shamans, chiefs, and tribal councils. Some systems have societies or sodalities of one kind or another—men's clubs, warrior societies, etc. Confederacies of tribes mark the upper limit of social evolution on preliterate levels.

The Agricultural Revolution rendered obsolete the fundamental institutions of primitive (preliterate) society—clan, tribe, and chief—and created a new type of cultural system that we call civil society, or the State. These latter systems have many more parts, and many more kinds of parts, than do systems on preliterate levels of development. Occupational groups, guilds of craftsmen, become numerous; societies are divided into dominant and subordinate classes, as we have already noted.

In the course of cultural evolution as in biological evolution, as the number of different kinds of parts increases, and the number of all parts increases, mechanisms of integration, regulation, and control are developed. This is of course necessary to hold a highly differentiated and specialized structure together. In the biological realm, the central nervous system is the integrative mechanism (see *The Integrative Action of the Nervous System* by Nobel Prizewinner Sir Charles Sherrington, 1906; 2d ed., 1947). In the cultural realm, the integrative mechanism is the State-Church: State and Church are the secular and ecclesiastical aspects of the mechanism of integration, regulation, and control of the cultural system (White 1959b, chap. 13). In some cultures the state aspect is uppermost; in others, the church is more prominent (e.g., Europe in the early Middle Ages).

We may distinguish, roughly, the following types of cultural systems with respect to mechanisms of integration: monarchy, feudalism, democracy, and communism. We must realize, of course, that the external world—physical, biological, or cultural—is under no obligation to adjust itself to our concepts and vocabulary. But we do need to have names if we wish to distinguish one thing from another and to talk about them. The terms cited above are the best (most realistic and meaningful) that we have at the present time. This means that we must free ourselves from the notion that there *is* something that *is* democracy, communism, etc. We have already encountered this difficulty among the anthropologists who tell us what culture "basically is." The distinction between words and things is fundamental; words are mere labels, and we apply them to things as we please. As John Locke observed many years ago: "We should have a great many fewer disputes in the world if words were taken for what they are, signs of our ideas only, and not for things in themselves" (*An Essay concerning Human Understanding,* 1690).

History has been concerned principally with the behavior of nations. To a great extent their behavior has been represented as due to its Great Men: "little was accomplished during that era because the nation had a weak king." Or, their behavior may be attributed to "the Greek (or any other nationality) mind," national aspirations, manifest destiny, or other verbalisms. I know of no scientific treatise on the behavior of nations comparable to scientific studies of monkeys and apes or the social insects.

The behavior of a nation is the expression of the integration of its components or vectors. Each as a magnitude, a force, and a direction. The expression of these syntheses constitutes the behavior of the nation.

nations are amoral

Only human beings *in society* are moral or immoral; only they have ethics.* Nonhuman species are neither moral nor immoral; they are amoral. Stars, planets, and their satellites are amoral. It is generally regarded as self-evident

---

* "Individuals can consider ethical requirements, they have consciences, but societies have none. . . . All societies, large and small, retain the character of wild hordes in considering every means good which

that nations *are* moral or immoral. The distinction usually made, however, is that "our" nation is moral; our enemies are immoral. The belief that nations are capable of ethical conduct derives from two sources: (1) people attribute the motives and values of human beings to nations; and (2) nations, as such, represent themselves to their human constituents as being animated by the highest, most noble, and purest motives.

A human being is one thing; a nation is another. A human being has nerves, glands, sheds blood. Social life and articulate speech have created ethical codes.* A nation is a different kind of system. It is composed of cultural elements: institutions, tools, weapons, ideologies. Nations are predatory and ruthless; the arena of international relations is a jungle in which cunning, guile, deceit, and raw, naked force prevail. Their "morality" is a device to conceal or to serve their purpose as the occasion dictates. One has only to read the history of the conquests of Peru, the West Indies, and Mexico, and the history of the acquisition of North America by the civilized nations of western Europe to observe them in their true colors: looting, pillage, genocide, subjugation, expropriation, and the doctrines of "the White Man's burden" and "manifest destiny" have been engraved on their record.† And in what respect are modern nations really different?

---

succeeds. Who would look for fidelity, veracity and consicence in the intercourse of the 'most civilized' states of the world? Lying and deceit, breach of confidence and betrayal is on every page of their history. . . ." Ludwig Gumplowicz (1899, pp. 146–47). Gumplowicz (1838–1909) was an Austrian economist and sociologist.

* "What is called conscience is thus . . . the reflex in the individual of the sanctions of society" Radcliffe-Brown (1934, p. 531).

† "Indeed, it is generally recognized that states oppose each other like savage hordes; . . . that no ethical law or moral obligation, only fear of the stronger, holds them in check; that neither right nor law, treaty or league, can restrain the stronger from seeking its own interests when the

Nations assiduously cultivate the belief that they are noble and righteous. This is an important process of nations as cultural systems: it is a way of promoting social solidarity and thus strengthening the system. It is a means of mobilizing moral human beings in support of the amoral nation's wars. In this, the Church plays a leading role; it presents the war to men and women, not only as a moral and noble venture, not merely *their* war, but a war divinely sanctioned. Wars thus become crusades (Dwight D. Eisenhower *Crusade in Europe,* 1948) if the people are Christians; a jihad if they are Moslems. Have not all wars of modern times been fought, and have not millions of men and women fought and died, for "Freedom" and "Liberty"? For the Fatherland? "For Man, for Country, and for God"?

the intelligence of nations

Nations are systems of a low order of intelligence. Simple reflex and tropism are terms that aptly characterize their behavior. Actually, it is as unjustifiable to use psychological terms ("intelligent," "stupid," etc.) in speaking of cultural systems as it is to use moral terms ("good," "bad," "just"). Only human beings are capable of morality, and only biological systems are capable of intelligent or stupid behavior. Stars are not intelligent; comets are not stupid. The situation is that we have no science of nations as cultural systems * and no appropriate vocabulary with which to talk about them. We are, therefore, obliged to borrow psychological terms and concepts if we wish to

---

opportunity is offered. . . . Plundering expedition, conquests, annexation, incorporation and war indemnities: these are the various forms in which the natural tendency of the state to augment its power and extend its authority is manifested" Gumplowicz (1899, p. 152).

* "Nations as Cultural Systems" (1968) was the first written statement of my thinking about cultural systems.

talk about the behavior of nations. But at least we can be clear as to what we are doing.

The lowest stage in the evolution of the behavior of living systems exhibits only simple reflexes and tropisms in which the reacting organism has no choice: its behavior is determined by its own properties and by the properties of things and circumstances in the external world, e.g., a positive reaction to food or a negative reaction to an injurious object: phototropism of sunflowers. On the second stage, that of the conditioned reflex, behavior is not determined directly by the intrinsic properties of the stimulus— reaction of the salivary glands of Pavlov's dog to the sound of a bell—but the organism still does not exercise choice; its behavior is determined by things and events over which it has no control. On the next stage (for which we have no adequate name) control does enter the picture: the ape uses a stick, in one way or another, to obtain food that is initially beyond his reach; he exercises discrimination and choice from start to finish. The fourth and last stage (so far, at least) in the evolution of minding is occupied by human beings only. Here are alternatives, discrimination, choice, and control and, in addition, meanings that cannot be comprehended with the senses alone (e.g., holy water; see White 1960).

If we think of behavior as a function of structure (which is a valid and fruitful way to regard it), then the evolution of behavior, or minding (White 1939), parallels the evolution of structure: the more complex the structure, the greater its capacity for advanced forms of behavior—from amoeba, to man. Intelligent behavior appears on the third and fourth levels of the development of minding. The correlation of behavior with structure is relevant—and may be illuminating—to a consideration of the behavior of cultural systems.

The simplest human societies known to science, such

as the hordes of aboriginal Australia, might be likened to
a colony of cells, or a drop of mercury: i.e., human beings
held together by ties of kinship and mutual aid; groups
having virtually no internal structure. Ralph W. Gerard, a
distinguished psychologist (1940, p. 411), speaks of
"nomad, self-sufficient Arab bands . . . at the sponge
stage of integration"; such a cultural system would be
limited to simple reflexes and tropisms. The behavior of
tribes, especially those with a council of chiefs, exhibits
some synthesis of factors involved in making decisions
(explicit or implicit), but it will still be on the level of simple reflex or tropism. Skipping over early forms of the
state, we turn to the most highly developed of modern nations.

The "highest stage of evolution . . . which has as yet
been reached by any [human] society," in the view of Sir
Julian S. Huxley (1940, p. 16), "is, by biological standards,
extremely primitive. It corresponds with a quite early stage
in the development of cerebral hemispheres—perhaps
higher than that of a fish, but certainly not beyond that
found in reptiles."

Gerard places advanced cultures of today on a still
lower level: "highly mechanized England, nobility gra-
dient and all, has perhaps reached the flat-worm stage"
(1949, p. 422; 1940, p. 411).

The cultural systems of western Europe since the days
of Charlemagne have varied considerably in complexity of
structure, in degree of integration, in subordination of
part to whole, etc.; the trend has not been invariably toward higher levels of integration. The development of relatively well-integrated nations, with power concentrated
in the institution of a monarch, followed the decentralization of feudalism and preceded the loosely integrated
capitalist cultures. All may be regarded as variants of a
fundamental pattern: the modern State.

To citizens who have been brought up to believe that nations are possessed of great wisdom, as they are supposed to possess great virtues, it may seem shocking—or even utter nonsense—to liken the most highly developed nation as being on a cultural level corresponding to the level of a fish in the biological scale of evolution—to say nothing of flat-worms. I know little about flat-worms, but I believe that modern capitalist cultures—and their post-capitalist successors—are "by biological standards" less highly developed and integrated than a fish. A fish is actually a very highly integrated system, whether compared with a starfish (which is not, strictly speaking, a fish) or with a modern nation.

Let us consider a class of modern national cultural systems, the "democratic" countries, i.e., those with representative government. And let us focus principally upon the United States: it is the nation that I know best and the one that would probably be of greatest interest to readers. Like all national cultural systems, the United States is composed of sectors, distinct parts of society or its economy. The major sectors comprise many subsectors. The agricultural sector, for example, may be divided into the cultivation of crops and the raising of animals. Each of these may be divided into parts: corn, wheat, cotton; horses, hogs, cattle, etc. The cattle sector is divided into dairy cows and beef cattle. The number of significant sectors and subsectors—from the standpoint of the economy and also of the election of congressmen—is tremendous. When we go from the agriculture industry to manufacturing, mining, transportation, communication, etc., and the professions—medicine, law, the clergy, acting, business, politics, the military, organized crime, etc.—we arrive at a very large number of significant parts. Each has a degree of autonomy, i.e., "self-ness." Each exerts economic influence; each is a source of political power.

The behavior of a nation is an expression of the coordination, the integration, and the synthesis of this multitude of parts, this myriad of vectors, economic and political. What ways and means does a nation like the United States have to accomplish these integrations and syntheses?

It can hardly be said, I believe, that the United States has a central nervous system. Speaking of modern societies Gerard says: "a coordinating central nervous system hardly exists. . . . In terms of transmissive coordination and adaptive amplification, our best societies today are at the nerve-net stage of the jelly-fish or perhaps entering the ganglionated central-cord stage of the flat-worm" (1940, p. 407).

The founding fathers designed the new nation so that a high degree of decentralization, or autonomy of parts, would be established, with virtually no means whereby the whole could achieve subordination of parts; the major components, i.e., states, had autonomy and independence in some contexts for decades. The national government was divided into three parts: the legislative, the executive, and the judicial; the Congress was divided into two relatively autonomous parts. If the House passed a bill the Senate could nullify it by refusing to support it.* If both Houses passed a bill the President could veto it. If the bill were passed over the President's veto, the Supreme Court could declare it unconstitutional. In the legislative field any congressman was free to propose legislation and seek support to pass it without reference to an overall

* It has been alleged that with regard to certain political issues—pure food and drug legislation, for example—there was a tacit agreement between House and Senate in matters of this sort: the House would pass a bill to pacify their constituents; the senate would then kill the measure by voting against it (congressmen are elected for a two-year term; senators, for a term of six years).

plan for the nation. Congress could authorize the expenditure of funds, but the President could impound them "in the national interest." If a court rendered an adverse ruling, the case could be taken to a higher court; one court could overturn the ruling of another. The government of the United States was deliberately organized—if one can speak of deliberate action at the level of a flat-worm or a fish—to render it as limited, as weak, and as ineffectual as the requirements of national survival would permit.

The consequence of this was natural and logical: the nation was not infrequently in conflict with itself, one part opposing another. The federal courts ruled that children must be bussed to schools in order to enforce racial desegregation. The chief executive opposed bussing and urged an amendment to the Constitution that would prohibit it. The Constitution gave Congress the prerogative of declaring war. But the President, who is Commander in Chief of the military forces, can *wage* war with out a declaration. The early 1970s witnessed one great part of the United States trying with all its might to extricate the nation from the wars in Indochina, while "the administration" stubbornly persisted in carrying on the war, and even ordered new bombing raids daily for many weeks after having achieved "peace with honor." A cultural system divided against itself cannot behave in a rational manner. In the biological realm we know of no parallel of such a system even among flat-worms.

But if the cultural system that is the United States has no central nervous system, it does have many mouths: not only the little mouths of its citizens, but the big mouths of the "leaders" of the nation. Senators, congressmen, ex-cabinet members, presidents of labor unions, generals and admirals, corporation executives, bank presidents, evangelists, baby doctors, and syndicated columnists, can and do speak out, in accents of wisdom and authority, about what course the nation should take.

Free expression of desires and needs of the various sectors of the cultural system is, of course, essential to a healthy social organism. But if this expression takes place at the top, where everyone is de facto on a par with the chief executive, the system is very poorly integrated and its behavior as a system can hardly be intelligent or rational. A system in which parts are free to speak for the whole is a system on a low level of integration; it has a number of ganglia but no central nervous system. A system that has a mechanism to synthesize the expressions of need and interest of the several sectors, and then to transmit this synthesis to the apex of the political structure, would be on a higher level of development and therefore more capable of integrated, effective, and even intelligent behavior. Many mouths and less than one central nervous system are not conductive to behavior of this kind.

The explanation of the extensive autonomy of parts and the unintelligent, reflexive, tropismatic behavior of a system like the United States is fairly simple. The core of the capitalist system was production of commodities for sale at a profit. The system required a maximum of freedom for entrepreneurs and a minimum of regulation and control (usually regarded as "interference") by government. The initial government of the United States was designed to provide a maximum of freedom for the youthful but vigorous capitalist system. Precapitalist, i.e., feudal, institutions that had been transplanted in the colonies—entailed estates, primogeniture, titles of aristocracy, an established church, etc.—were uprooted, giving the capitalist system an open field, without fetters, for the first time. This form of government, plus the vast and rich territory that this system appropriated, brought capitalist culture to its highest level of development in the world. It is no wonder that American institutions have been extravagantly extolled for a century or more.

The ability of a biological organism to behave as a unit does not require a high degree of integration; the lowest forms of life can do that. It is not a question of what kind of behavior is possible on successive levels of integration. Specifically, we are trying to distinguish a class of systems that are capable of "intelligence," which we have already defined. We have already declared modern nations to be nonintelligent systems. Let us now supply a few examples of their behavior.

During World War II, the two great English-speaking nations declared that the conflict must be terminated by unconditional surrender of their enemies. Their principal foe was Communism—despite the fact that the Soviet Union was on their side. At the conclusion of the war, the victorious powers—Great Britain and the United States in particular—undertook to reduce Germany and Japan to a condition of helplessness. Thus, they removed from the arena of international competition the two nations who had been the principal means of keeping communism in check: Germany in the West, Japan in the East. The military emasculation of these two nations opened the way to the emergence of China as a Communist nation and to the preeminence of communism in Eurasia.

United States policy toward China after the war unquestionably did much to strengthen the Communist regime there. United States aid to Nationalist China and to the impotent has-been Chiang Kai-shek, was no deterrent to communism. On the contrary, it gave the Communist Chinese a tremendous propaganda advantage: the presence of "American imperialism" on their very doorstep probably did more to inspire, integrate, and solidify China than any internal situation could have done.

Having been a prime mover in humbling and disarming Germany and Japan, the next reflex undertook to restore these nations to something like their former greatness—in the West against the Soviet Union; in the East, against China.

But this was not all. Germany was divided into two parts: West and East; Capitalist and Communist. Berlin, the capital, was completely surrounded by Communist Germany but not a part of it. It was divided into four sectors, each one to be under the authority and administration of one of the four principal victorious powers of World War II: Great Britain, the United States, France, and the Soviet Union. It would be hard to imagine a situation more conducive to international friction and strife; one can almost imagine a misanthropic, deranged genius conceiving of this arrangement. More realistic, however, is to think of it as the expression of many simple reflexes that, put together, was something like the mentality of *Alice in Wonderland.*

the united states and war in vietnam

A nation is a thermodynamic system, as we have noted before. If it has sufficient energy to expand, it does so. It extends a pseudopodium toward a fertile valley or plain, a warm water seaport, a Northwest Passage, a site for an interoceanic canal, a Gibraltar. Like an amoeba, it may surround and ingest its prize.

The state of Vietnam was formed in July 1949; it was recognized by the United States in February 1950. In June 1950, President Truman announced that he was sending a 35-man Military Assistance Advisory Group to Indochina to "advise" troops in the use of American weapons. In December 1950, the United States signed a Mutual [*sic*] Assistance Agreement with Vietnam (smaller than the state of Oklahoma). After the 1954 partition, President Eisenhower in October offered economic aid to South Vietnam. In February 1955, the United States agreed to train the South Vietnamese army.

December 14, 1961, President Kennedy declared that the United States was prepared to help the republic of South Vietnam "preserve its independence." Eight days later Specialist 4 James Davis was killed by the Viet Cong; President Johnson later said that Davis was "the first American to fall in defense of our [sic] freedom in Vietnam." In the summer of 1964 the alleged attack upon two American destroyers by North Vietnamese torpedo boats took place; President Johnson ordered immediate retaliatory attacks. Congress passed the Tonkin Resolution giving the President power to "take all necessary measures to repel any armed attack against the forces of the United States and to prevent further aggression."

In December 1962, the United States had a military force of 4,000 men in Vietnam. By 1967 the figure had increased to 474,300 men—1,500 more than United States troop strength in Korea during the Korean War. United States troop strength in Vietnam reached its maximum in February 1969, with a total of 542,500 men.

United States military casualties reckoned from January 1, 1961, to January 5, 1967, were 6,664 dead and 37,738 wounded. By April 1969, total United States deaths had risen to 33,641, surpassing the number killed in the Korean War. As of October 9, 1971, 45,572 Americans had met their death in Vietnam; 301,936 had been wounded.

Peace talks between the United States, North Vietnam, and the Viet Cong began in Paris in May 1968. Shortly after his inauguration, President Nixon announced his plan to "wind down the war." In April 1970, however, U.S. forces and those of South Vietnam invaded Cambodia. In February 1971, South Vietnamese troops, with U.S. air and artillery support, invaded Laos. On October 26, 1972, a ceasefire agreement had been reached. In January 1973, President Nixon announced that he had obtained "Peace with Honor." The fighting continued. In February 1973, Mr. Nixon ordered the bombing of Cambodia, and for several months huge American planes dropped thousands of tons of bombs upon this tiny nation (area: 69,898 sq. mi., the size of the state of Missouri), against widespread protest in the United States and the efforts of the Congress to stop the fighting. Finally, after Congress had moved to cut off funds for military action in Indochina, the bombing of Cambodia was terminated.

The war in Vietnam was the longest war in United States history. Why was it fought? A number of explanations were offered: by the President, by members of Congress, and by others who took it upon themselves to speak for the nation. "To prevent a Communist take-over in Vietnam"; to defend "our freedom in Vietnam," as President Johnson once put it. None of the explanations was convincing or satisfying to most American people. Finally, explanations degenerated to a lame "U.S. commitment." Not infrequently, a war is waged in the interest of a powerful financial or industrial sector of the nation—to obtain control of oil, tin, rubber, or to gain or expand markets. But no such rational claim was ever noticeably put forth during the war in Indochina. The great majority of Americans never knew why their nation was waging a war, 8,000 miles from their homeland, at the expense of thousands of American lives and billions of dollars of taxpayers' money.

The story of the United States war in Indochina is the recitation of one reflex after another. First the "advisers," then the troops. More troops were needed to protect those already there. A squadron of superbombers was based in neighboring Thailand. A huge fleet of warships, including aircraft carriers, hovered along the coast. There was never a declaration of war. . . . The United States got into the Vietnam war much as the sabre-tooth tiger got into the La Brea (tar) pits in Los Angeles. . . . No better evidence of the lack of a central nervous system—or at least a cerebrum—could be found than the conflict between the President of the United States and the Congress during the bombing of Cambodia—after the President had announced his "Peace with Honor."

We should pause here to say a good word for reflexes and tropisms. These forms of behavior have made survival possible for all species of plants and animals below the level of mammals. They have made it possible for organisms to distinguish the beneficial from the injurious, and both of these from things of neutral value. Reflexes and tropisms have, at times, served nations well, also. But this is not intelligence.

the energy crisis

In 1973 the United States suddenly discovered that it was in an "energy crisis"—an acute shortage of petroleum.

The lowest living organism knows when it is in the presence of danger; no species could long survive without this ability. On a higher level of development, animals can detect danger at a distance: they are able to recognize signs of danger—the sight, odor, cry, or spoor of a predator. This enables them to take measures of defense or flight before the predator seizes them. It may reasonably be assumed that even the tiny-brained dinosaur could do this. But the United States, the leviathan, does not see danger from afar and take measures to cope with it; it discovers that it is in danger only after the crisis has overtaken it.*

---

* After Arab countries placed embargoes on shipmnts of oil to pro-Israeli countries after the war of October 1973, "spokesmen" and the press tended to give the impression that the energy crisis—or "crunch," as they preferred to call it—was due to "blackmail" on the part of the Arab nations, and there was considerable talk about repirsals. But this was gross misrepresentation. The energy crisis was upon us and recognized prior to the Arab-Israeli war. Furthermore, the United States received only a relatively small percent of its crude oil from the Middle East prior to the war. And finally, World War II had made the United States

I present herewith a review of some of the highlights of the history of the production and consumption of petroleum in the United States up to the year 1969 when Richard M. Nixon was inaugurated President of the United States. This brief sketch is a partial inventory of information available to the legislative and executive branches of the United States government for years prior to 1969.

The "Petroleum Age" began in 1859 when E. L. Drake drilled a producing well in western Pennsylvania. Production increased very rapidly after the invention of the automobile. Consumption increased with accelerating velocity: in the decade 1937–1947, one-half of total world production of petroleum was consumed; 97 percent of this total was consumed between 1900 and 1947 (Hubbert 1950, p. 172). The United States portion of world production was fairly constant at about 64 percent from 1910 to 1940, after which it declined greatly: to 52 percent in 1950, 33 percent in 1960, and 22 percent in 1969 (*Statistical Abstract of the United States,* 1953, p. 734; for 1971, p. 644).

Production of crude petroleum in the United States increased from 7.8 trillion BTUs in 1940 to 18.9 trillion BTUs in 1969—an increase of 142 percent. Consumption increased at a much greater rate: from 7.5 trillion BTUs in 1940 to 28.4 trillion in 1969—an increase of 279 percent. This required, of course, a great increase of imports: from 178 millions of barrels (42 gallons) in 1950 to 514 million barrels in 1969—189 percent in less than two decades. Exports declined during this period from 35 million barrels

---

keenly aware of deprivation of much needed materials from abroad, and another war in the Middle East was not unexpected.

The Christian Science Monitor (Nov. 23, 1973, Western edition) quoted a Nobel Prizewinning economist at Harvard University, Wassily Leontief, as accusing the Nixon administration and the oil industry of "attempting to shift the blame to Arab nations" for what he termed their "gross miscalculations" in planning for U.S. energy needs" (p. 14).

in 1950 to 1 million in 1969 (*Statistical Abstract of the United States,* 1971, pp. 496, 644).

Motor vehicle registrations in the United States increased from 49.2 million vehicles in 1950 to 105.1 million in 1969, an increase of 112 percent in less than two decades. Motor fuel consumption (by passenger vehicles, trucks) increased from 40,280 millions of gallons in 1950 to 88,122 millions of gallons in 1969, an increase of 119 percent (*Statistical Abstract of the United States,* 1971, pp. 533, 538).

The population of the United States increased 94 percent in the fifty-year period 1919–1969.

In 1952, Eugene Ayres and Charles A. Scarlott (*Energy Sources, the Wealth of the World*) observed that the rate of exhaustion of reserves of oil in the United States was greater than in other oil-producing countries (p. 34).

The story up to this point is, in short, increased demand, decreased supply.

World Power Conferences were held periodically beginning in 1924. Innumerable studies of oil production, consumption, and reserves were published in the decades prior to 1969. Palmer C. Putnam, an engineer, a graduate of the Massachusetts Institute of Technology, was engaged by the Atomic Energy Commission to make an exhaustive study of the world's energy resources and requirements; *Energy in the Future* (1953) was his report. Dr. M. King Hubbert's "Energy from Fossil Fuels" was published in 1950. The Fourth World Power Conference (1950) published a review of "Energy Resources of the United States" (*Transaction,* vol. 1, 1952). In 1951, Dr. James Bryant Conant, a distinguished chemist and president of Harvard University, expressed the belief that the era of liquid fossil fuel would come to an end about the close of the twentieth century and that anxiety about coal resources would be on the increase; he believed that solar energy might become the "dominating factor in the production of industrial power" by the year 2000 (1951, p. 3848). Ayres and Scarlott sounded a warning in 1952: "The problem of energy for the United States is not one of the future; it is upon us now." And, anticipating the Middle East component of the energy crisis of 1973, they stated that "the rate of production in the Middle East is expected to be high long after the rate in the United States has declined." (1952, pp. 31–32).

Information concerning energy needs and resources was abundant and accessible in the decades prior to 1969; much of it was published yearly by the United States Government in *Statistical Abstract of the United States.* The energy situation had been made clear by competent studies time after time. Warnings had been issued. How was it then that the United States, as a nation, with all its advisory councils, data-gathering bodies, congressional hearings, etc., should suddenly discover that it was in a crisis?

The answer, we believe, lies in our analysis of the structure of the cultural system that is the United States. It is composed of numerous disparate parts, but a central mechanism for synthesizing information is crude, if not lacking entirely. In biological terms, the nation has no central nervous system. With the awful realization that the nation was on the verge of a crisis, if not already well into it, prominent people (and some not so prominent) by the score—cabinet members, senators, congressmen, governors of states, mayors of cities, "spokesmen" for oil companies, consumers—turned to radio and television to inform, counsel, and exhort the citizenry. Again: many mouths but not much cerebrum.

The Christian Science Monitor headlined its issue of November 23, 1973 (Western edition): "Too many voices in energy policy confuse U.S. public . . ." An article by the business/financial correspondent quoted a Senate source as saying: "No one here [in Washington] knows who is running the government's energy policy, with the result that the White House speaks with many voices. A Nixon administration official was equally blunt: 'There is not a coherent effort going on to learn the real dimensions of the energy crisis.' Why? 'There is no strong person in charge and no organization, *no institutional framework,* to administer energy policy' " (p. 1; emphasis added).

In the weeks and months that followed, the United States, "the greatest nation in the world," presented a sorry spectacle, writhing in the many-tentacled grip of a situation that it had not foreseen and for which it had no plan; doing this, trying that, exhorting the citizenry ("To save energy we urge you to keep your electric blankets turned down low"); inept, fumbling, ineffectual.

the head of the state

Whether he be an hereditary monarch, an elected president, or a dictator who has come to power by force, the head of a state is the point at which the vectors of the cultural system (the nation) intersect and where syntheses of vectors are effected and expressed. Each vector has its magnitude and power, i.e., its ability to influence the achievement of syntheses.

It might be inferred that the President of the United States must be an exceptionally able man, a man of wide knowledge and understanding, in order to administer the affairs of a great nation. Many citizens of the Republic believe that he is, indeed, such a man. But an examination of the evidence leads to a quite different conception of the head of the state.

The American president need not be a man of exceptional ability. The history of this office makes it clear that many who have occupied it have been very ordinary, even mediocre, persons. As James Bryce observed many years ago in *The American Commonwealth,* "How many of the presidents would be remembered at all had they not been elected to that office?" And, "the only remarkable thing about them is that being so commonplace, they should have climbed so high" (1910, 1, p. 77). Chapter 8 of *The American Commonwealth* explains "Why Great Men are not Chosen President." The caliber of occupants of the White House since *The American Commonwealth* was first published in 1888 remains substantially unchanged. Speaking of President Coolidge, H. L. Mencken remarked that had he not become president he would have made a good county superintendent of schools.

To have been a high-ranking army officer might seem to be one of the lesser qualifications for the office of president, but in addition to Generals Washington, Grant, and Eisenhower, four major generals and two brigadier generals (some by brevet) have been elected to this office.

The head of a great state may possess only a superficial understanding of the cultural system of which he or she is the geometric apex. Queen Victoria "was unaware of two significant facts," wrote George Dangerfield in a review of Hector Bolitho's *The Reign of Queen Victoria:* "that she was not the ruler of England, and that she had not the vaguest idea who the real rulers were. She could not, for example, even have guessed at the forces [i.e., vectors] which received their outward expression in figures like Joseph Chamberlain and Cecil Rhodes" (1948, p. 18).*

---

* "Thou dost not know, my son, with how little wisdom the world is governed," Count Axel Oxenstierna, in a letter to his son (1648). Oxenstierna was a Swedish statesman and chancellor under Gustavus Adolphus. (This quotation is most probably originally from *Bref . . . til Grefve J. Oxenstierna, åren 1642–1649: med Tellägningar.* Utgifne af C. C. Gjörwell. 2 band. Stockholm, 1810–19. I find no reference to a translation of this work. It seems likely that White is quoting from a secondary source. BD.)

A professor of history who became President of the United States, Woodrow Wilson, had more insight:

> The masters of the government of the United States are the combined capitalists and manufacturers of the United States. It is written over every intimate page of the records of Congress, it is written all through the history of conferences at the White House. . . .
>
> Suppose you go to Washington and try to get at your government. You will always find that while you are politely listened to, the men really consulted are the men who have the biggest stake—the big bankers, the big manufacturers, the masters of commerce, the heads of railroad corporations and of steamship corporations.
>
> The government of the United States at present is a foster-child of the special interests. It is not allowed to have a will of its own. (1913, pp. 57–58)

Wilson was very much aware of the vectors of his cultural system.

Abraham Lincoln realized that it was social, economic, and political forces, not he, that determined the course of events: "I claim not to have controlled events, but confess plainly that events have controlled me. Now, at the end of three years' struggle, the nation's condition is not what either party, or any man, devised or expected" (telegram to A. G. Hodges, Frankfort, Kentucky, April 4, 1864. See Lapsley 1906, p. 118.)

Adolf A. Berle, Jr., a learned and perspicacious student of cultural systems (e.g., *The American Economic Republic*), asserted that the federal government's assumption of responsibility for the "functioning of the economic system" of the United States in the crisis of 1933 was "an innovation of the first order. . . . The political act was the work of President Franklin D. Roosevelt" (1965, p. 95). But, he goes on to say that "most of the conceptions, elements, forces and institutions [vectors] used and regrouped [synthesized] in the new order *were already in existence prior to 1933,"* and, although the "political act was the work of President Roosevelt, similar assumption [of "responsibility for the function of the economic system"] *probably would have been forced on any President holding office at that time"* (ibid., emphasis added).

The insight and understanding of Lincoln and Wilson are exceptional among American presidents; the naivete of Queen Victoria is not a handicap to a head of state. But neither are insight and understanding necessary; as a matter of fact, if asserted and defended, they might well be a handicap in the give-and-take, log-rolling, pork-barrel politics of the American state; a case in point: Woodrow Wilson.

No President of the United States could possibly become sufficiently informed, concerning the hundreds of issues that come before him, to form intelligent and wise decisions. But he does not need to have the information nor to make the important decisions. There are scores of mechanisms for gathering information, debating policy, and arriving at decisions: the cabinet, congressional committees, the National Security Council, the Central Intelligence Agency, and ad hoc "task forces" to do his work. He need not, and usually does not, write his own speeches. A myriad of cultural forces—economic, political, military, medical, etc.—must come together and interact to reach a decision.* This decision may not, and perhaps usually does not, represent a consensus of the participants in the interaction; it may simply emerge as the expression of the most powerful force at that time. It is the President's function to express not the "will of the

* "Out of the conflicting pressures from interest groups of all types [such as labor, manufacturing, government] comes legislation, public policy, and, albeit vague, a commonly accepted definition of the general welfare and the national purpose" (Steigerwalt 1964, p. ix).

people" but the strength of the most powerful vector or vectors. Indeed, it has been alleged that a powerful business and industrial interest, a single corporation, can successfully oppose the federal government. The persistence of "organized crime" and the multi-billion-dollar drug traffic would seem to point to the same conclusion.

In addition to particular forces that influence the behavior, not only of the President, but also of the nation, there is public opinion, that vast and powerful tropism of the body politic. Lord Bryce was much impressed with the importance of public opinion in the United States—"the mind and conscience of the whole nation. . . . that determines [sic] the direction and the character of national policy" (1910, 1:6). More than sixty years have elapsed since the second edition of *The American Commonwealth* was published. During this time the news media have expanded greatly with the advent of radio and television. The magnitude of this vector is greater than it was in Bryce's day and there is no question about its influence. But it is not merely that public opinion exerts an influence upon the nation; public opinion is itself shaped, given content and direction, by various economic and financial interests and their lobbies, such as public utilities, the packing industry, the railroads, farmers' and labor organizations, the American Medical Association, the American Bankers Association, the Federal Council of Churches, etc., etc. This was the situation in Bryce's day as well as now. Public opinion is made on the one hand, and exerts its influence on the other. But powerful, it is.

Returning to the matter of presidential advisers, it may be observed that in many instances the advice given is of a low order, i.e., unrealistic. We recall President Franklin D. Roosevelt's almost frantic attempt to obtain advisers equal to the needs of the time. As a particular example of the bumbling and ineffectual counsel that a body of advisers may offer to the chief executive, let us consider the President's Council of Economic Advisers of the early 1970s. Inflation was, no doubt, their principal problem; unemployment and allocation of production quotas were secondary.

The crux of the problem confronting them was: how can the system of free enterprise be made to function effectively without destroying the free enterprise system? To ask this question is to answer it: a system regulated by price and wage controls is no longer a free enterprise system. The nation was deeply committed by word, thought, and deed to the free enterprise system. But the exigencies of the situation made it clear that governmental controls were necessary to prevent chaos or collapse. Understandably, the attempt to reconcile these conflicting ways of life posed a problem too difficult for the Council of Economic Advisers to solve.

In the first place, there was no consensus among economic experts regarding the cause or cure of inflation. Measures to curb inflation proposed by some experts were declared to be futile by others—or, even to be aggravations to the situation. Price controls imposed upon one sector of the economy threw other sectors out of joint. Measures to curb rising food prices adversely affected industries engaged in food production. Wage controls without controls of rents and interest rates were protested. The measures taken were ad hoc, attacking trouble spots without attempting—or being unable—to grapple with the economic system as a whole.

Members of the Council are obliged to function in a "gravitational field" where they are alternately pushed and pulled by numerous powerful economic and political forces. Their performance is feeble and at times irrelevant to the fundamental issues facing them. Some of their predictions might as well have been derived by haruspicy as by cogitation and compromise. In fact, the Council of Economic Advisers reminds one of the augurs and haruspices of ancient Rome, and of Cicero's observation that it was marvelous that one haruspex could look another in the face without laughing (Cicero, *de natura deorum,* chap. 71).

If anyone in the nation really understood the cause of inflation, and knew what measures would effectively curb it, he could not be identified among the unorchestrated experts. The problem is a culturological problem: it has to do with the structure and functions of a cultural system. Both structure and functions belong to the real world and are subject to the principle of cause and effect. "If such and such is the cause then such and such will effect a cure."

This is not an admission of free will or the proposition that "man can control his culture." Knowledge and understanding are themselves cultural material, and of necessity ideas and beliefs react with and upon economic systems. There was a time when the cause and cure of certain diseases were not known or understood. Increase of knowledge and understanding in the field of medicine, *as cultural phenomena,* acted upon these diseases and brought them under control; it is culture acting upon culture, one part exerting influence upon another. Culturological knowledge and understanding of inflation do not exist (or, at least, they are not identifiable) in our culture at the present time (1975). And, of course, culturological theory cannot be effective without facts to work with. What the significant facts and processes are is not apparent at the present time.

If the President wields great power, it is the power of the state; he is its instrument, or the instrument of a dominant vector or vectors. The cultural system that is a nation is a crude and clumsy affair as compared with a highly integrated system such as that of a fish. The methods employed by it in the selection of a President also are crude and more or less haphazard.* This leaves room for the expression of idiosyncrasies of the chief executive. Adolf Hitler was chosen and installed as the head of the German state by powerful industrial, financial, and political vectors. As a rule, once a nation has placed a man in the position of head of state it is difficult to remove him. An attempt to remove Hitler from office by assassination failed. Four American presidents have been assassinated. President Andrew Johnson was impeached by the House of Representatives; he was tried by the Senate, which did not muster the two-thirds majority necessary to convict him. (It should be noted, in this connection, that the prime minister of Great Britain is not the head of the state; he is the head of his political party.)

The head of state must be receptive to the influence of others. This is as true of men who come to power via a military coup as it is of one who is elected by the citizenry. *L'état, c'est moi* is a delusion. It is obvious, of course, that no individual could come to high office without the assistance of others. Receptivity to influence is a *sine qua non* of any potential office holder, be he big or little, the head of a military junta, or the elected representative of the people. One who is impervious to influence, e.g., a stout, stubborn man of principles, would make syntheses of vectoral influence impossible—the well-known monkey wrench in the machinery. The ideal president would be a

---

* "Society is in bitter need of better mechanisms for selecting its leaders. . . . When proper leaders . . . can be selected by devices which are more dependable and objective than are the accidents of family, rhetoric, ambition, and other circumstances which today frequently toss undesirable individuals to the apex of the power pyramid. . . ." (Gerard 1942, p. 84).

man of no principles whatever, like an automatic pilot of an airliner. And, it has been alleged, some occupants of the White House have come close to this ideal. This theory throws light on the widespread belief among the electorate that "all politicians" are lacking in honesty and integrity. Congressmen, for example, function in a great network of economic, political, regional, occupational, and even familial, vectors in which compromise is essential. What Congressman A or Senator B may believe in and want to do as a person, must in many, many instances be subordinated to what he must do as a part of the political process. And, as remarked above, individuals who are unwilling or unable to respond to the influence of others stand little or no chance of being elected or of becoming a dictator.

It might be inferred from the thesis presented here that the head of the state can do nothing on his own, nothing completely independent of the matrix of economic and political forces within which he functions and has his being. This inference is more than implied here, and, I would say, it is a sound one. The following paragraphs are borrowed from my article, "Nations as Sociocultural Systems" (1968):

> There is a device with which scientific theories can be put to a test without recourse to laboratory experiments or to instrumental observation and measurement of things and events in the external world. This is to imagine what would be the effect upon the theory in question *if* certain events took place. For example, if iron refused to oxidize under normal conditions, or would not melt despite high temperatures. Or suppose that cows gave birth to lambs or that chickens hatched from duck eggs. What effect would this have upon science's conceptions of reproduction and inheritance? Suppose that an

aboriginal tribe in Australia should suddenly begin to talk French, or amuse themselves with quadratic equations. Or that the citizens of the United States should abruptly refuse ever to touch an automobile again. We would have to revise some of our fundamental notions about the nature of the man-culture system.

Now let us suppose that the President of the United States, or the head of some other state, should do something, in his role as chief executive, purely and absolutely on his own. It is a bit difficult to think of something that would meet these requirements; almost everything that he does, or might do, would involve the demands, desires, pressures, advice, of others. But we can think of a few that come close to an act uninfluenced by others. Suppose the President of the United States should abruptly and without warning issue an executive order declaring that this nation should immediately and forthwith embark upon a program of thorough, complete and unilateral disarmament. We can think of no organized interest in the United States that would advise him to do this or even to suggest such a monstrous thing: the nation would very quickly fall flat on its face if such a policy were carried out. And any individual who might suggest such a course of action would have much less chance of communicating with the President than an assassin would have of killing him.

Or, let us suppose that the President should issue an executive order that would abolish the institution of private property—immediately and thoroughly so that all natural resources, all means of production, all corporations, banks, insurance companies, etc., were to become socialized. These are examples of the only kind of thing that the chief executive could do on his own unaffected by the sociocultural system of which he is an integral and crucial part.

It is as difficult to imagine the chief executive of the United States doing things of this sort as it would be to imagine the chicken issuing from a duck egg, or the Australian aborigines speaking French. As a matter of fact, it is *impossible* for an occupant of the White House to do a thing like that—unless. . . . unless he had taken leave of his senses. What *would* probably happen if he actually did order, in his official capacity, the socialization of all wealth or immediate and complete unilateral disarmament? We believe the answer can be predicted with tolerable accuracy. A first thought (i.e., intellectual reflex) would be that the President would be impeached, but this seems unlikely; to take such action would imply responsibility on the President's part. Only an utterly irresponsible—and probably insane—man could do the things we have imagined. What probably would happen would be somewhat as follows: His wife and some friends would summon a physician who would give the President a sedative. His wife would pack a suitcase or two and the chief executive would be removed, quickly and discreetly, to a nice sanitarium in some undisclosed place. Then the machinery of government would declare that he was medically incapable of discharging the duties of his office and he would be replaced according to law. In some less democratic countries he might simply be taken out and shot (pp. 17–18).

the emergence of the concept of cultural systems

AS we have pointed out, both in the Prologue and, from time to time, within the body of this essay, much of what we have to say has been anticipated by students of "Man and his Works"; many have sensed that customs (folkways), institutions, and ideologies constitute a distinct order of phenomena, logically independent of man (i.e., man, per se, cannot be used as an explanatory device by means of which variations of this distinct order (culture) can be made intelligible). Many have sensed that culture "has a life of its own." Tylor, Durkheim, and others have maintained that cultural phenomena can be treated scientifically just as physical and biological phenomena can; the conception of a science of culture was made explicit by Gustav Klemm over 100 years ago.

Like much of our intellectual culture, a concept of cultural systems was made explicit by the ancient Greeks: Plato's *Republic,* Aristotle's comparative study of some 158 constitutions of city states, etc. We shall not undertake a detailed study of the ancestry of this concept through the work of the early Church Fathers or the philosophers of the Middle Ages and the Renaissance. We shall take as our starting point the relatively modern concept of a society as an organism, for this, in my opinion, was the immediate ancestor of the concept of cultural system.

The literature expounding the conception of a society as an organism is voluminous and involved.* It was part of the groping attempt of its day to realize the concept of cultural systems, but its premise—a society *is* an organism—only led scholars down a dead-end road.

The era of the social organism school was, roughly, the last quarter of the nineteenth century. It was considered worthy of the attention of sociologists during the first few decades of the twentieth century, however: the principal textbook in the Department of Sociology at the University of Chicago—*Introduction to the Science of Sociology*—edited by Robert E. Park and Ernest W. Burgess (1921), contained a four-page review of "The Social Organism: Humanity or Leviathan?" in its introductory chapter. *The Encyclopaedia of the Social Sciences,* published between 1930–1934, contained an article on "Social Organism" by Gottfried Salomon. But the *International Encyclopedia of the Social Sciences,* published in 1968, did not carry an article on this subject.

Among the most prominent exponents of the social organism school were Paul Lilienfeld, a Russian of German descent (*Zur Verteidigung der Organischen Methode in der Soziologie,* Berlin, 1898); Albert Schäffle, a German professor and statesman (*Bau und Leben des socialen Körpers,* 1875–76), René Worms, a French professor and permanent secretary of the International Institute of Sociology and editor of the *Revue international de sociologie* (*Organisme et société,* 1896), and J. Novicow, a Russian (*La théorie organique des sociétés, defense de l'organicisme,* Paris, 1899).

Confusion arose from the fact that scholars of this school presented human society as a biological organism. Both adherents of this view and its critics agreed that this

* Reviews of the literature, with ample bibliographies, may be found in Pitirim Sorokin (1928); Gottfried Salomon (1934); Harry Elmer Barnes (1925).

was the premise of their theory. But the adherents protested that that was not what they meant, according to Sorokin (1928, p. 208, n.35), who quotes them on this point. They continued to elaborate and defend the concept, however. "Even among French sociologists," says Salomon (1934, p. 140a), "the conception of society as a real [sic] organism continued to be expounded." Those who espoused the organism theory of society busied themselves with finding homologues to the heart, circulation of the blood, stomach, lungs, arms, hair, head and what not (Sorokin 1928, p. 206). Paul Lilienfeld likened the cellular division into endoderm, mesoderm, and ectoderm to the division of the social organisms; J. K. Bluntschli regarded the state as masculine, the church as feminine (ibid.). Opponents of the theory pointed out that consciousness in society existed in its component individuals, whereas the cells of a biological organism lacked consciousness. They also noted that in society the individual was free to move about, even to the extent of entering another society, whereas the cells of a biological organism were fixed in place. The dialogue was virtually fruitless.

Herbert Spencer is generally regarded as an exponent of the theory of the social organism. This is due largely, no doubt, to the answer he gave to the question raised in part 2, chapter 1, of *Principles of Sociology,* namely, "What is a Society?" Chapter 2 is devoted to the answer: "A Society is an Organism." Sorokin mentions Spencer twice in his chapter on "the Bio-Organismic School" but sets him apart from its principal exponents such as Lilienfeld, Schäffle, and Worms. Park and Burgess include Spencer in their discussion of the social organism, but note that in Spencer's thinking there is a "cardinal difference" between a social organism and a biological organism (p. 27). Salomon also mentions Spencer more or less in passing, in his encyclopaedia article, "Social Organism."

"Having thus considered in their most general forms the reasons for regarding society as an organism [growth, mutually dependent parts, etc.]," says Spencer, "we are now prepared for following out the comparison in detail" (p. 462). He cites, as an analogy, "the channels which carry . . . blood-corpuscles and serum" and channels which carry "men and commodities." In chapter 9, "The Regulating System," he compares the systems employed by biological organisms with those of social systems.

At the outset of his discussion of this subject, Spencer asks if "the attributes of a society" are *in any way like those of a living body* (emphasis added). His answer is "yes," because "the permanent relations among the parts of a society are analogous to the permanent relations among the parts of a living body" (p. 448). This is a far cry from saying that a society is a biological organism. He points out "cardinal differences" between the two kinds of organism: "In the one case, consciousness is concentrated in a small part of the aggregate. In the other, it is diffused throughout the aggregate. . . . As, then, there is no social sensorium, the welfare of the aggregate, considered apart from that of its units, is not an end to be sought. The society exists for the benefit of its members; not its members for the benefit of society" (pp. 461–62).

Spencer emphatically repudiates "the belief that there is any special analogy between the social organism and the human organism" (p. 592, n.):

> "let it be once more distinctly asserted that there exist no analogies between the body politic and a living body, save those necessitated by mutual dependence of parts which they display in common. . . . I have used the analogies elaborated, but as a scaffolding to help in building up a coherent body of sociological inductions.

Let us take away the scaffolding: the inductions will stand by themselves" (pp. 592–93).

One wonders why Spencer deliberately constructed a situation from which he then had to fight his way out. "You perceive the force of a word . . . the right word." said that master of English prose, Joseph Conrad ("A Familiar Preface" to *A Personal Record*). If Spencer had only used the word *"system"* instead of *"organism,"* he would have spared a generation of sociologists and laymen much fruitless and sometimes passionate argument. Apparently Spencer was wedded to the triad inorganic, organic, and superorganic. Had he used *"physical"* (or *"inanimate"*), *"biological,"* and *"cultural"* for his triad the history of sociology would have been different. "Early writers," said the eminent chemist Frederick Soddy, "when they really meant what is now called energy, often used the term force . . . [this] confused the issue and retarded the growth of science to an almost incalculable extent" (1912, p. 19).

There was another semantic difficulty also: the word "organism" was taken to mean biological organisms and nothing else. This was no doubt due to the notion, still found in scholarly circles today, unfortunately, that a word "means just what it means"—that is, the meaning is inherent both in the word and in its referent: Adam called the animal a horse because it *was* a horse. The notion that the meanings of words are determined by usage is making its way today—but slowly.

"An atom is now an amazingly complicated organism," said Robert Andrews Millikan, a Nobel Prizewinning physicist, "possessing many interrelated parts" (1931, pp. 46–47). "An organism, whether or not a living one, is an integrated *system* composed of interrelated units," says Gerard (1949, p. 419) "molecules of water vapor crys-

tallized into a snowflake are interrelated and organized.
. . . *the snowflake is an organism*" (emphases added). An
organism is "an entity having an existence independent of
or more fundamental than its elements and having distinct
members of parts whose relations and powers or properties are determined by their function in the whole" (*Webster's*, 3d ed.).
    An organism may, therefore, be inanimate, biological,
social, or cultural.

expansion of the scope of science

Science—its assumptions, premises, point of view, purpose, and techniques of interpretation—began with as-
tronomy. It extended its scope, bit by bit, during the centuries: first focusing upon the inanimate realm, then upon
the biological—anatomical, physiological, and psychological. During the latter part of the nineteenth and the early
part of the twentieth century came a realization, and an
appreciation, of the fact that significant determinants of
behavior lie beyond the individual, that society is a major
determinant of human behavior as well as bones, glands,
and nerves. Sociology, as a distinct focus of science,
came into being with the clear recognition of this fact
(White 1947). To be sure, this had been sensed by earlier
thinkers like Thomas Hobbes (1588–1697), who thought of
"a Commonwealth, or State as that great Leviathan, which
is but an artificial man." It was not by chance that "social
organism" and sociology were welded together in the
thought of Herbert Spencer.
    With the discovery of *society* science crossed a frontier
and entered a new field of exploration and cultivation. Sociology bloomed and flourished, especially in the United
States. Albion W. Small (1854–1926), one of the pioneers,

began one of his books with the words "In the beginning was the Group." *

Science had made a great advance in moving from the individual to *society,* but it failed to discover the all-important field of *culture*—all-important in that (1) it was peculiar to the human species, and (2) it constituted the most powerful of all determinants of *human* behavior. The really significant thing about the behavior of man was not that it took place within society but that it was a response to a stimulus peculiar to Homo sapiens. If social life were the significant thing then monkeys, apes, fish, ants, and plants were in the same category as man. As a matter of fact, Park and Burgess's *Introduction to the Science of Sociology* included material on domestic animals, the societies of ants, and plant communities.

Culture had been "discovered" at least as early as the 1850s and the concept had been made explicit by Gustav Klemm. Edward B. Tylor, a contemporary of Spencer, entitled chapter 1 of *Primitive Culture* (1871) "The Science of Culture." Spencer was certainly well aware of the work of Tylor; they had a running debate in the journal *Mind* through several issues. Spencer went to great pains to show that his sociology was not derived from Auguste

* The reader may be interested to know, and be somewhat reassured by knowing, that I had close personal contact with sociology throughout the 1920s. I took courses in sociology with Franklin H. Giddings, William F. Ogburn, and others at Columbia University in the early 1920s. I took the courses in ethnology/sociology by William I. Thomas at the (old) New School for Social Research (New York) at the same time. In 1924 I went to the University of Chicago to work for a doctorate in sociology. There I took courses with Albion W. Small, Robert E. Park, Ernest W. Burgess, Ellsworth Faris, and others. It was there that I became acquainted with *Introduction to the Science of Sociology,* edited by Park and Burgess (and affectionately called by some students, "The gospel according to St. Park").

Comte, and he may have avoided borrowing from Tylor for the same reason. Spencer never grasped the concept of culture. His "superorganic," which is believed by many to be Spencer's equivalent of culture, was defined so as to include nonhuman species, and therefore not the culture of Klemm, Tylor, and American anthropologists (up to about 1930, at least).*

Sociology, as an ideological vector in modern cultural systems, could develop only its inner potentialities: the group, society, social interactions, etc. It was bound within these limits and therefore could progress only within them; it could not cross over into Canaan and cultivate the fertile field of culture. This was to be done by others.

It was anthropologists who discovered culture, said A. L. Kroeber (1936, pp. 331, 333). And, I would add, it has been anthropologists who have cultivated this field (although many anthropologists have not yet discovered it). The concept of social organism played a significant role in the transition from sociological science to culturological science.

* I have great admiration and profound respect for Herbert Spencer. I believe that he was one of the greatest minds in the Western world in the nineteenth century. But, he failed to grasp two concepts that I regard as fundamental in the sciences of man: the conception of the uniqueness of man's mind and the conception of culture. It seems almost incredible that a man of Spencer's penetrating intelligence, with his profound grasp of all the sciences and his rigor of thought, should have failed in these two fundamental respects. He was familiar with the work of his contemporary, E. B. Tylor, in which the uniqueness of man is made crystal clear and the concept of culture is expounded at length and in a lucid manner. Spencer's failure to realize the uniqueness of man's mind might have been due to his evolutionist penchant for seeing series of infinite gradations instead of sudden leaps. Also, he might have been influenced by the great prestige of Charles Darwin who argues, in chapters 2 and 18, *The Descent of Man,* that man is merely a more intelligent anthropoid rather than the possessor of a new and unique mind.

the "social organism"

The social organism becomes a "collective organism" in the philosophy of Auguste Comte (1798–1857). The human individual was an abstraction: he existed only in participation in the life of society. Park and Burgess summarize Comte's view as follows:

> Thus the individual man was, in spite of his freedom and independence, in a very real sense 'an organ of the Great Being' and the great being was humanity. Under the title of humanity Comte included not merely all living human beings, i.e., the human race, but he included all that body of tradition, knowledge, custom, cultural ideas and ideals, which make up the social inheritance of the race, an inheritance into which each of us is born, to which we contribute, and which we inevitably hand on through the processes of education and tradition to succeeding generations. This is what Comte meant by the social organism (Park and Burgess 1921, p. 25).

This is obviously a culturological conception. It is remarkable that it should have preceded the "classic" literature of the social organism school of Lilienfeld, Schäffle, et. al.

The concept of social organism becomes indistinguishable from the concept of cultural system—except for terminology—in the philosophy of Sidney Webb (1859–1947), an English economist and socialist, one of the founders of the Fabian Society. We quote at some length from his remarkable essay, "Historic," one of several published in 1889 in *Fabian Essays in Socialism,* edited by G. Bernard Shaw:

> slowly sinking into men's minds all this while [during the preceding century of industrial and political evolution] was the conception of a new social nexus, . . . It

was discovered (or rediscovered) that a society is something more than an aggregate of so many individual units—that it possesses existence distinguishable from those of any of its components. . . . A community must necessarily aim, consciously or not, at its continuance as a community; its life transcends that of any of its members; . . . Though the social organism has itself evolved from the union of individual men, the individual is now created by the social organism of which he forms a part: his life is born of the larger life; his attributes are moulded by the social pressure; his activities, inextricably interwoven with others, belong to the activity of the whole. Without the continuance and sound health of the social organism, no man can now live or thrive. . . . His conscious motive for action may be, nay, must be, individual to himself; but where such action proves inimical to the social welfare, it must sooner or later be checked by the whole, lest the whole perish through the error of its member. . . .

The French nation was beaten in the last war, not because the average German was an inch and a half taller than the average Frenchman, or because he had read five more books, but because the German social organism was, for the purposes of the time, superior in efficiency to the French (pp. 50–52).

Everything that Webb said about the social organism could be said about cultural systems. Still, there exists a fundamental difference between the conception expressed in sociological terms and its culturological counterpart: Webb was a sociologist; sociology is the science of the interaction of human beings and of societies formed by this interaction. Culturology is concerned with the interaction, not of human beings, but of cultural elements and culture traits (customs, institutions, codes, technologies, ideologies, etc.). This difference may seem small and unimportant to some; a number of sociologists have declared that it is merely splitting hairs. But the difference is tremendously important: focusing upon culture, a distinct order of phenomena, making it the object of scientific scrutiny and interpretation, is a far cry from focusing upon individual human beings *or* societies of human beings *because the behavior of peoples is a function of their respective cultures.* The proper study of mankind is not *man,* but culture. The concept of social organism provided a bridge, a transition, from the level of sociological conception and thought to the higher level of culturology.

There was a trend toward the conception of social organism among professional social workers of the United States during the closing years of the nineteenth century. "These younger men and women shared the 'growing belief that human society is an organism, under a law of development. . . .' " according to Frank Dekker Watson, a professor of sociology and social work at Haverford College (1922, p. 334). Jane Addams, a prominent social worker of this era, used the term "social organism": "they insist that it [Christ's message] shall seek a simple and natural expression in the social organism itself" (1960, p. 13); "the Social organism has broken down through large districts of our great cities" (ibid., p. 10). The point of view expressed by the concept social organism was in marked contrast to the individualistic spirit of laissez faire among social workers of earlier years.

Émile Durkheim uses the term "social organism" rather freely, both in *The Division of Labor* (1893) and in *The Rules of Sociological Method* (1895). But we wish to call attention to his conception of society that, incidentally, is remarkably like that of Comte:

> It is not true that society is made up only of individuals; it also includes material things, which play an essential role in the common life. The social fact is some-

times so far materialized as to become an element of the external world. For instance, a definite type of architecture is a social phenomenon; it is partially embodied in houses and buildings of all sorts which, once constructed, becomes autonomous realities, independent of individuals. It is the same with the avenues of communication and transportation, with instruments and machines used in industry or private life. . . . (1897, pp. 313–14, Eng. trans. 1951).

The conception here is culturological rather than sociological.

Karl Marx used the concept of social organism in *Capital* in characterizing trading nations—and perhaps elsewhere: "Trading nations, properly so called, exist in the ancient world only in its interstices, like the gods of Epicurus in the Intermundia, or like Jews in the pores of Polish society. Those ancient social organisms of production are, as compared with bourgeois society, extremely simple and transparent" (1912, p. 51). G. D. H. Cole (who wrote a book entitled *What Marx Really Meant*) seems to say, in his article "Socialization" in the *Encyclopaedia of the Social Sciences,* Vol. 14, 1934, that Marx's thesis of socialization implies a concept of social organism.

the concept of cultural systems in American ethnography and ethnology

The concept of cultural systems was probably implicit in some studies of tribal cultures in the early years of American ethnography; the systemic character—the organization of interdependent parts to form a unity—may well have impressed itself upon the ethnographers. But this conception was seldom, if ever, made explicit. In later years, the period during which Franz Boas was very influential, there was not only a lack of recognition, or acceptance, of the conception of cultural systems, but a pronounced negative attitude toward such a conception.

Among early ethnographers who made comprehensive studies of tribal cultures, Lewis H. Morgan's *The League of the Iroquois* (1851), Matilda Coxe Stevenson's *The Zuni Indians* (1901–1902), and *The Omaha Tribe* by Alice Fletcher and Francis La Flesche may be cited as notable examples of studies in which the concept of cultural system may well have been implicit.

Franz Boas (1858–1942) and many of his prominent students took a negative attitude toward the conception of systemic organizations of culture. Boas had an intense preoccupation with particular traits and their diffusion from tribe to tribe. The culture possessed by a tribe was therefore, in his view, a congeries of disparate traits rather than a systemic organization of them. Robert H. Lowie, one of Boas' most prominent students, objected to the use of the term "system" by W. H. R. Rivers in Rivers' discussion of kinship and social organization because it "connects with it the notion of some organic connection among the constituent elements. This certainly holds to some, but only to a very limited extent. . . . The truth of the matter simply is that there is *no* organic connection but a chance historical association. . . . Any particular 'system' is almost certainly always the resultant of a number of psychologically diverse and in the beginning historically distinct factors" (Lowie 1917b, p. 269). Ruth Benedict, a disciple of Franz Boas, expressed a similar view: "It is, so far as we can see, an ultimate fact of human nature [*sic*] that man builds up his culture out of disparate elements, combining and re-combining them; and until we have abandoned the superstition [*sic*] that the result is an organism functionally interrelated, we shall be unable to see our cultural life objectively" (1923, pp. 84–85).

Perhaps the most extreme statement of an anti-systemic conception of culture is to be found in the closing paragraph of Lowie's *Primitive Society* (1920): "that planless hodge-podge, thing of shreds and patches called civilization. . . . the chaotic jumble."

To Boas, also, culture appeared to be chaotic. He speaks of the "chaos of [tribal] beliefs and customs" in an early report of his field work on the Northwest Coast, observing that "the student stands aghast before the multitude and complexity of facts that confront him." (Boas 1898b, pp. 3–4). Boas began his study of the Kwakiutl Indians in 1886; fifty years later he was working with a Kwakiutl informant in New York. His published writings on this tribe exceed 5,000 printed pages. Yet, with all this, he did not "complete a single, large-scale portrait of a tribal culture, not even of his beloved Kwatiutl" (Lowie 1947, p. 313); the "chaos of beliefs and customs" proved to be too much for him; the systemic character of Kwakiutl culture eluded him (White 1963, pp. 52, 55).

During the decade 1910–1920, it was the fashion to publish studies of tribal cultures piecemeal. In making this observation I do not mean to disparage these studies. An ethnographer must do his work when and as he can and with the resources available to him. The circumstances of publication also, might encourage small monographs rather than larger ones that could accommodate a culture as a whole. But the fact remains—however it may be explained—that a number of anthropologists during this period published several papers on various aspects of a culture, leaving it to the reader to piece them together as best he could to form a conception of the culture as a whole.

Lowie, for example, published at least ten papers on various aspects of the culture of the Crow Indians be-

tween 1912 and 1924: * on their social life, military societies, religion, Sun Dance, Tobacco Society, myths and traditions, material culture, art, minor ceremonies, the Crow
and Village Indians, etc. Similarly, Clark Wissler published
papers on the culture of the Blackfoot: ceremonial bundles, material culture, social life, mythology, Sun Dance,
societies and dance associations, etc., between 1908 and
1916. Volume 11 of *Anthropological Papers of the American Museum of Natural History,* 1916, dealt with "Societies of the Plains Indians." In 984 pages, it contained se-
venteen articles by five authors, fifteen of which were by
three authors. All this is in sharp contrast with *The Life
and Culture of the Hupa,* by Pliny Earl Goddard (1903),
and *The Northern Maidu,* by R. B. Dixon (1905), which
provided at least a snapshot of the culture as a whole.
But, even when a monograph attempted to cover the entire culture, it often presented it in discrete segments—
habitat, social life, economics (which usually was technology), ceremonies, mythology, etc., with virtually no discussion of how the parts formed an organic whole.

from "planless hodge-podge" to order

To one who perceives the world about him only with his
senses, the impression made upon him might well be one
of chaos "before which one stands aghast," as Boas put
it. But when reflective thought grapples with a myriad of
sense impressions, a multitude of things and events each
of which is in actuality unique, order emerges, be it naive
or sophisticated. "Everything goes by fours," a Dakota Indian told an ethnographer: "there are four directions; four
divisions of time: the day, the night, the moon, and the

* These papers by Lowie, and Wissler's papers mentioned below, were
published in the Anthropological Papers of the American Museum of
Natural History.

year; four kinds of things that breathe: those that crawl, those that fly, those that walk on four legs, and those that walk on two legs; four kinds of gods . . . ; four periods of human life . . . ; and finally, mankind has four fingers on each hand, four toes on each foot and the thumbs and the great toes taken together make four. Since the great spirit caused everything to be in fours, mankind should do everything possible in fours" (Walker 1917, pp. 159–60). The diversity represented by the bat that flies, the whale that lives in the ocean, the mole burrowing in the ground, the swift antelope of the plains, the ape of the jungle, and man, himself, was formerly regarded as part of a divine plan; science finds order in a grand pattern of evolutionary development. It was to be expected, therefore, that when and as the point of view of science was brought to bear upon the myriad of diverse cultural phenomena, order would emerge.

The first significant step taken in American ethnology of the twentieth century was "Psychological Types in the Cultures of the Southwest," by Ruth Benedict, a paper presented at the Twenty-Third International Congress of Americanists in New York, in September 1928.* Benedict distinguished two types of cultures in aboriginal North America: the Dionysian and the Apollonian (terms borrowed from Friedrich Nietzsche). The first was characterized by ecstasy, frenzy, excess, orgiastic behavior, etc.; the latter by sobriety, restraint, self-control. Pueblo cul-

* The concept of culture areas was, of course, a means of ordering cultural phenomena, of distinguishing types of culture correlated with distinguishable geographic regions. This concept goes back at least to Albert Gallatin's *Notes on the Semi-Civilized Nations of Mexico,* etc. (1845). It was subsequently used by O. T. Mason (1896), Clark Wissler (1917), A. L. Kroeber (1939), and others. But this concept is hardly relevant to the subject of cultural systems.

tures were Apollonian, "islanded in the midst of predominantly Dionysian cultures" (p. 15).

From what has gone before it might not be apparent to the reader why I regard this essay by Benedict as a step in the direction of a conception of cultural systems: Benedict's conception of psychological types and my conception of cultural systems may seem to be miles apart, as indeed they are. But they have one thing in common, and this, an important feature: *both look at the culture of a people as a whole.* Otherwise, our respective treatments differ radically. Benedict explains, or makes intelligible, the culture of the Pueblos in terms of a psychological type rather than explaining the psychological type in terms of the culture—the mode of life. She states that the "cultural situation" of the Apollonian Pueblos "is in many ways hard to explain" (p. 23). But "a clue is to be found in a fundamental psychological set which has undoubtedly been established for centuries in the culture of this region [the Southwest]." Without an understanding of this psychological set "the cultural dynamics of this region are unintelligible" (p. 23b). How then does she explain the "psychological set?" By "the typical choices of the Apollonian [which] have been creative in the formation of this culture, they have excluded what was displeasing, revamped what they took" (p. 13b). Not a word about how a sedentary, intensive horticultural way of life might predispose a culture toward one kind of psychological type; or how a nomadic, bison-hunting, warring way of life might tend toward another kind of "psychological set." But, let us not lose the point of all this: to Benedict cultures are not planless hodgepodges, chaotic jumbles; they are ordered structures with inner harmonies. We are not concerned here with the soundness of her conception or the validity of her conclusions—or with the question of whether or not some other interpretation of the cultures of the Southwest might have been "better" than the one she used. The special significance of her essay derives from its object, its goal: to see cultures as coherent wholes rather than a fortuitous aggregation of traits thrown together by the pointless process of diffusion.

It was in "Psychological Types in the Cultures of the Southwest" that Benedict "first developed" her "major insight . . . that culture can be seen as personality writ large," according to Mead (1968, p. 49); it "laid the groundwork for all her later significant contributions." Benedict's essay made an impression upon Boas, with whom she was closely associated. In 1930 Boas wrote of the "most instructive manner" in which Benedict had treated "the 'Apollonean' formal pattern of the Pueblos" that exerted "a strong influence upon them through behavior." He also speaks of the "strong influence of the pattern. . . . in social organization and religious ritual," all of which he regards as "integration of culture" (Boas 1930, pp. 101–2).

Kroeber and Kluckhohn (1952, p. 151) tell us that Boas "gave his first definition . . . of culture at the age of seventy-two." He first explicitly acknowledged the integration of culture at the same age.

In 1932 Benedict followed her essay on psychological types with a paper on "Configurations of Culture in North America" (Mead regards Benedict as "the originator of the configurative approach to culture," 1968, p. 48). In the beginning of this essay Benedict harks back to a position taken in *The Guardian Spirit in North America.* But she now reverses herself completely with regard to the "superstition" of the organic unity of cultures. Tribal cultures are still "overwhelmingly made up of disparate elements fortuitously assembled from all directions by diffusion," but now these traits are "over and over again in different tribes integrated according to very different and individual patterns. . . . order is due to the circumstance that in these societies a principle has been set up [*sic*] according to which the assembled cultural material is made over into consistent patterns in accordance with certain inner necessities that have developed within the group" (1932, p. 2). She is talking about cultural systems and how they behave, although her wording does not make this explicit.

In "Configurations of Culture in North America" Benedict reviews the psychological types, the Apollonean and the Dionysean, and expands the documentation of examples of configurations, but nothing new of theoretical significance is presented. "Cultural configurations stand to the understanding of group behavior in the relation that personality types stand to the understanding of individual behavior. . . . This is a reading of cultural from individual psychology" (pp. 23–24). "The cultural configuration builds itself up [*sic*] over generations, discarding . . . the traits that are uncongenial to it" (p. 26). Once "psychological sets . . . have become institutionalized, they can shape the resulting cultures" (p. 4). The extent to which Benedict "psychologizes" cultures is indicated by the following: "It seems to me that cultures may be built solidly and harmoniously upon fantasies, fear-constructs, or inferiority complexes and indulge to the limit in hypocrisy and pretensions" (p. 26).

Here again, we are not concerned with the difference between psychological (psychiatric) and culturological points of view. We are not here concerned with the soundness of Benedict's "diagnoses" of variously configurated cultures and we certainly are not going to descend to the kind of criticism that says, in effect, "she should have done it differently—or done something else." "Configurations of Culture in North America" is a significant step in the effort to deal with cultures as unified wholes.

In 1934, Ruth Benedict's *Patterns of Culture* was published. In this book she presents portraits of three cultures: the Pueblos of New Mexico, the Dobu Islanders off the southern coast of eastern New Guinea, and peoples of the Northwest Coast of America (primarily the Kwakiutl tribe). These portraits (and I think this term is very fitting; they are more like paintings than scientific analysis and description) are set in a frame of considerable discussion: psychological, sociological, ethnological. She speaks of the concept of the social organism and its turbulent history. She does not adjudicate the dispute about its validity, but she does say this: "It is obvious that the sum of all the individuals in Zuni make up a culture beyond and above what those individuals have willed and created. The group is fed by tradition; it is 'time-binding.' *It is quite justifiable to call it an organic whole"* (p. 231, emphasis added). Thus Benedict has come full circle from her characterization in 1923 of the idea of "an organism functionally interrelated" as a "superstition" that should be abandoned.

Papa Franz, as his women students affectionately called him, was impressed. In his Introduction to *Patterns of Culture,* he speaks of "the desire to grasp the meaning of a culture as a whole" approvingly (p. xvi). Benedict's study "brings out clearly the forms of integration in various types of culture" (p. xvi). But the old habit of particularism is still strong in Boas: the patterns are so diverse that they "do not lend themselves profitably to generalizations" (p. xvii).

The sharp break that Benedict—one of Boas' closest professional associates (Mead 1959, p. 3410, speaks of her as "Boas' left hand")—made with the point of view and techniques of interpretation often, and justifiably, called "Boasism" is noted by Boas' first Ph.D. at Columbia, A. L. Kroeber. In his review of *Patterns of Culture,*

Kroeber said: "No approach is farther than this from the customary analytic one of Boas" (1935, p. 689).

American ethnology had come a long way from the endless trees of Boasian ethnology (not to mention uncountable branches and twigs) to a vision of a forest. The "drift," to use one of Sapir's favorite words, was toward a conception of cultural systems.

values and cultural systems

ANOTHER movement in American ethnology, that of regarding cultures as systemic wholes, took place in a concern with values. After a few tentative—and unrelated—beginnings in the 1940s, the conception of cultures as value systems was launched upon a grand scale and in a concerted manner in 1949 primarily under the leadership of Clyde Kluckhohn. The principal object of this movement was, naturally, the scientific study of values, the possibility of such a study having been previously denied. But the effect of a concern with values was to oblige the ethnologist to come face to face with, and accept, the conception of cultures as systemic wholes. Thus, another step was taken by American ethnology toward the fundamental and simple conception of cultural systems.

Among American ethnologists, Melville J. Herskovits, disturbed by the impact of World War II upon the American way of life, published "On the Values in Culture" in 1942. In 1949 Kroeber presented a paper, "Values as a Subject of Natural Science Inquiry," before the National Academy of Sciences. In the same year Clyde Kluckhohn asserted, in *Mirror for Man,* that "'no tenet of intellectual folklore has been so damaging to our life and times as the cliche that 'science has nothing to do with values'" (p. 285). In this statement Kluckhohn "defined a major challenge and frontier of social research," in the opinion of Vogt and Roberts (1956, p. 25).

Also, in 1949, an ambitious six-year program of research in the area of values and value systems, supported by the Rockefeller Foundation, was launched by the Laboratory of Social Relations, Harvard University. Its primary objective was to study five communities in the American Southwest in order to determine the significance of values in the cultural differentiation and similarity among them. Many academic departments, museums, and universities rendered advice and assistance, and a very large number of scholars were engaged in the project. Sixty-five field workers and twenty-five analysts are listed as having participated in values research in this region between 1936 (the year Kluckhohn did his first field work among the Navaho) and 1952 (Kluckhohn 1951, pp. vii–ix; Vogt and Albert 1966, pp. vii–x). A list of field workers and analysts may be found in a prefatory page in *Navaho Veterans* (Vogt 1951). John M. Roberts was coordinator, Vogt deputy coordinator, of the project.

The five ethnic groups to be studied were the Zuni Pueblo Indians, a community of Navaho Indians, a Mormon community, a community of Catholic Spanish-Americans, and a community of Protestant-Anglo-American homesteaders from Texas. All of these groups were located in a relatively small area south of Gallup, New Mexico. Thus, a very favorable "laboratory situation" provided an excellent opportunity to study a variety of cultures in terms of their own structures and processes. The study of values thus became, in effect, a study of cultural systems.

The application to the Rockefeller Foundation for financial support understandably emphasized the importance of the proposed study: "There is general agreement among thoughtful people today," it said, "that the problem of 'values' is of crucial importance [*sic*], both practically and from the point of view of scientific theory" (Kluckhohn 1951, p. vii). Perhaps the most notable study of an entire community to emerge from this program was *Modern Homesteaders: The Life of a Twentieth Century*

Frontier Community (Vogt 1955); it dealt with the Protestant Anglo-American homesteaders from Texas. Other studies focused upon a single sector of a culture, studied, of course, against the background of the culture as a whole. *Zuni Law: A Field of Values* (1954), by Watson Smith and John M. Roberts and *Navaho Veterans; A Study of Changing Values* (1951), by Vogt, exemplify this type of study (a list of publications of the values study and manuscripts in press and in preparation in 1954 is to be found in the prefatory pages of *Zuni Law*). All of the above mentioned studies, with the exception of *Modern Homesteaders,* were published in the *Papers of the Peabody Museum* of Harvard University.

what is a value?

It would not be easy to find another word whose meaning is so indefinite and uncertain as the word "value." The author of "The Concept of Values," Robert M. Williams, Jr., says that the term "may refer to interests, pleasures, likes, preferences, duties, moral obligations, desires, wants, needs, aversions and attractions and *many other modalities of selective orientation*" (*International Encyclopedia of the Social Sciences,* p. 283; emphasis added). Casting about for something not included by the term, Williams comes up with "sheer reflex behavior . . . [such as] a knee jerk." In some contexts a value appears to be the incentive that initiates action; in others it is the goal for which one strives. In still other contexts it is merely a pervasive feeling, such as the Hopi attitude toward snakes or the Navaho attitude toward the dead. "It is very doubtful," says Williams, "that any one descriptive definition can do complete justice to the full range and diversity of recognizable value phenomena" (p. 283). Thus, "value" may refer to virtually any human act, attitude, feeling, quality, or goal. Curiously enough, no one seemed distressed by this multi-faceted ambiguity. Perhaps it gave them a sense of freedom: "value is whatever you think a value is, or ought to be."

The understanding of values is more difficult than the foregoing would suggest. "Values are intangible," according to Kroeber and Kluckhohn (1952, pp. 172–73); "values are not observable any more than is culture," says Vogt (1951, p. 6). As was the case with culture, the question arose "Are values therefore unreal?" Kroeber and Kluckhohn hasten to assure the reader that values are indeed real: they "are part of nature, not outside it. They are the products of men, *of men having bodies* [*sic*] and living in societies" (1952, p. 172).*

the achievement of the values study

What might one reasonably expect from the labors of scores of field workers and analysts over a period of several years, in a project administered by the Social Sciences Laboratory of a great university, generously supported by the Rockefeller Foundation? My answer would be "much more than was achieved in terms of their own premises and concepts": the concept of value proved to be virtually sterile as an explanatory device.

Modern Homesteaders represents perceptive observation and intelligent, competent research. It is vivid and

* Although Kroeber and Kluckhohn were joint authors of *Culture: a Critical Review of Concepts and Definitions,* the portions of this work dealing with values bears the imprint of Kluckhohn rather than that of Kroeber, in my opinion. Kluckhohn's interest in values as a scientific and philosophical problem was much greater than that of Kroeber, as is evidenced by their respective bibliographies. Furthermore, I have discovered that a number of passages in *Culture, a Critical Review* are identical, word for word, with passages in articles published by Kluckhohn. This is not said in criticism by any means, nor is there any suggestion of plagiarism. It was perfectly ethical—as well as economical—for Kroeber and Kluckhohn to use material previously published by one or both of these authors.

substantial ethnography. But not because of the use of the concept of values; quite the contrary, this concept was intrusive. The monograph would have been better without it. The same might justifiably be said of *Zuni Law* and *Navaho Veterans*. Let us turn to an exposition of the use of the concept "value" and an evaluation of the fruit of this concept, by the coordinators of the Values Study themselves: Vogt and Roberts.

We believe that "A Study of Values" (Vogt and Roberts 1956, pp. 25–31) provides a fair exposition and appraisal of the "values study." The cultures of the five communities studied differ because they are activated and directed by different values ("Differences in culture can thus be related to differences in values" p. 29). If cultures are to be explained in terms of values, how do Vogt and Roberts explain values and why one community has certain values while another has different values? Answer: they don't explain this; they say that each people "chooses" its values: "the forming and choosing of values is a central concern of all men and societies" (p. 25).

Vogt and Roberts do not avail themselves of cultural (culturological) explanations of the differences among the five communities. Each has its own powerful cultural tradition, a mode of life and thought handed down from generation to generation for centuries. Even the two Indian communities, Zuni and Navaho, had markedly different cultural traditions. And to say that the Mormon community differed from the Protestant Anglo-American community because it had "different values" is to contribute nothing whatever to an understanding of this difference. They were confronted with five different cultural traditions that they could have used effectively as explanatory devices. But they rejected this substance for the wraith of "value." They have gone back centuries in the development of modern thought in the Western world to the days when phlogiston was the best explanatory device avail-

able to physicists. The concept of value as used by Kluckhohn, Vogt, and Roberts reminds one of the old explanation: "Opium puts one to sleep because of its dormitive
powers." People behave as they do because of the values
they have chosen.

But, if the concept was sterile as a means of explaining
the behavior of human societies or their cultures, the "values study" of Kluckhohn et al. was not without merit. In a
word, its significance lay in the attempt to grasp cultures
as organized wholes:

> values provide the only basis for the fully intelligible
> comprehension of culture, because the actual organiza-
> tion of all cultures is primarily in terms of their values.
> . . . the picture of a culture without reference to its val-
> ues . . . becomes a meaningless assemblage of items
> having relation to one another only through coexistence
> in locality and moment—an assemblage that might as
> profitably be arranged alphabetically as in any other
> order; a mere laundry list (Kroeber and Kluckhohn 1952,
> p. 173).

The resemblance of the above to the developing ethnology of Ruth Benedict is so close that one might suspect
collusion; perhaps it might be an example of Kroeber's
"stimulus diffusion." Benedict also protested against
viewing culture as a fortuitous assemblage of traits. She,
too, felt the need of a concept that would enable her to
grasp a culture and to comprehend it as a whole. Hence
her psychological types, her configurations, her patterns
of culture. She, too, like Vogt and Roberts, said that
various peoples "chose" or "selected" their patterns or
values (see *Patterns of Culture,* pp. 237, 254).

And so we can locate the "values study" on the unfold-
ing map of American ethnology: it lay, like the work of
Benedict, along the road toward the concept of cultural
systems.

functionalism

IN 1926 Brownislaw Malinowski (1884–1942) came to the United States for a few months' visit. In 1931 Alfred Reginald Radcliffe-Brown (1881–1955) arrived in the United States to occupy a professorship in anthropology at the University of Chicago; he remained at that institution until 1937 (with time out as visiting professor at Yenching University, Peiping, in 1935). Through these scholars American anthropologists were personally introduced to functionalism, so to speak, although some were familiar with their writings before they came to America.

The essence, the fundamental nature or characteristic, of functionalism may be stated briefly and simply: human societies and their respective cultures exist as organic wholes composed of interdependent parts. The parts cannot be fully understood apart from the whole and the whole must be understood in terms of its parts, their relationships to one another, and to the sociocultural system as a whole. To put it even more succinctly as Herbert Spencer did: "A society is an organism [system]."

The introduction into American ethnology of a philosophy markedly different from the one that had enjoyed a near monopoly for some thirty years gave the impression of novelty and led to the belief that the conceptions and point of view of functionalism were new and radical. Rhoda Metraux, the author of the biographic article on Malinowski in the *International Encyclopedia of the Social Sciences,* asserted that "Malinowski was the originator of a functionalist approach to the study of culture" (p. 41). "As far as I know, in this country [England] Malinowski regarded himself as the

Founder of the Functionalist School" wrote Brenda Z. Seligman (1950b), the wife of Charles G. Seligman. Malinowski himself once spoke of his "humble capacity of godfather and standard-bearer of the functionalist method" (1932, p. xxiv), and accepted "responsibility for the *label* 'functional',", but adds that *"the principles themselves, and the method, are as old as empirical and comparative anthropology,* and they are best represented in some of the work of the previous generation of anthropologists—in the writings of Westermarck and E. B. Tylor, of Grosse and Durkheim" (1930b, p. 13; emphases added). Lowie (1937) has said that "Bachofen is an aggressive functionalist" (p. 41), "emphatically a functionalist" (p. 43). Bohannan (1965, p. viii) declares that Lewis H. Morgan was "as much a functionalist as an evolutionist." Fenton (1962, p. xviii), also, considers Morgan a functionalist.

We would derive functionalism from two sources: philosophical ethnology and ethnographic field work. First and foremost in the former category I would place Herbert Spencer. "The two writers who most specifically directed the attention of social anthropologists towards functional analysis were Herbert Spencer and Emile Durkheim" in the opinion of Evans-Pritchard (1951, p. 51), a statement with which I would heartily agree.

Turning now to field work, I would begin with the English scientific expedition to Torres Straits in 1898, led by A. C. Haddon. In saying this I do not rule out functionalist insights or explicit recognitions of the organic unity of cultures by ethnographers prior to 1898. But with the Torres Straits expedition a continuity of functionalist insight and point of view begins. First of all there was Haddon: "under his influence a school of ethnology arose which aimed at studying 'savage' man *in situ*" (B. Z. Seligman 1950a, p. 305). W. H. R. Rivers was a member of this expedition; later he did extensive field work in Melanesia. In his presidential address, "The Unity of Anthropology," Rivers said "the unity which is so apparent to one who studies simple cultures in the field is a necessary feature of any society. . . . This unity is of the same kind as that of the living organism, the activity of every part of which contributes to the completeness and harmony of the whole" (1922, p. 13). C. G. Seligman, also, was a member of the Torres Straits expedition. Malinowski was a student of Seligman, and it was he "who launched Malinowski's expedition to the Trobriands" (B. Z. Seligman, 1950b). "It was his [Malinowski's] experience in the field combined with theoretical knowledge that led Professor Malinowski to formulate in 1926 his 'functional method'," according to Haddon (1934, p. 124). Radcliffe-Brown was a student of both Haddon and Rivers. Thus, the ethnological fruit of this famous expedition was both rich and varied.

But field work alone does not of necessity produce a functionalist point of view, though it seems almost obvious and necessary that this result must ensue from field experience. We have already quoted Margaret Mead's statement that "when one works with a living culture this wholeness is part of one's everyday experience" (1959, p. 204). But Franz Boas was able to work with the Kwakiutl for more than fifty years without portraying their culture as an organic whole. Perhaps it was his obsession with particulars and with diffusion that kept him from doing this.

the core of functionalism

Malinowski says: "Culture must not be treated as a loose agglomeration of customs, as a heap of anthropological curiosities, but as a connected living whole. . . . The functional method insists on the recognition of the process of culture as a process *sui generis*, . . . culture is alive, it is dynamic, all its elements are interconnected, and each fulfills a specific function in the integral scheme" (1929, p. 864a).*

For Radcliffe-Brown: "The newer social anthropology. . . . looks at any culture as an integrated system and studies the functions of social institutions, customs and beliefs of all kinds as part of such a system. . . . By the function of an institution I mean the part it plays in the total system of social integration of which it is a part" (1931a, pp. 154, 152).

The concept of systems is not only explicit but emphatic in Radcliffe-Brown's thinking. In his presidential address "The Study of Kinship Systems," before a meeting of the Royal Anthropological Institute, Radcliffe-Brown remarks: "You will perceive that by using the word "system" I have made an assumption, an important and far-reaching assumption; for that word implies that whatever it is applied to is a complex unity, an organized whole" (1941, p. 3). After asserting that a science of culture is impossible, Radcliffe-Brown says: "You can study culture only as characteristic of a social system. Therefore, if you are going to have a science, it must be a science of social systems" (1957, p. 106).

reception of functionalism by
american anthropologists

As one who had a keen interest in, and ample opportunity to observe, functionalism,† I would summarize the reac-

---

* It may be noted that Malinowski entertained another conception of functionalism, also: "Functionalism is in its essence, the theory of transformation of the organic—that is, individual needs into derived cultural necessities and imperatives. The individual, with his physiological needs and psychological processes, is the ultimate source . . . of all tradition, activities, and organized behavior" (1939, 938–64).

† When Malinowski was in Chicago in 1926, Professor Fay-Cooper Cole asked me to assist him by taking him to places where he wanted to go and by being of service in any other way that I could. This I did gladly; it

tion of "established" anthropologists as follows: (1) some resisted functionalism, criticized it, belittled it; (2) many tried to show that American anthropology had been practicing functionalism all along.

Leslie Spier, discussing Boas' *Tsimshian Mythology,* observed: ". . . one may understand why the majority of anthropologists have come to view every culture as a congeries of disconnected traits, associated only by reason of a series of historical accidents, the elements being functionally unrelated. . . . It will also be understood why the doctrine of the 'functionalists' (Radcliffe-Brown, Malinowski) is invalid to the majority of anthropologists" (1931, p. 455). We have already cited Benedict's anti-functionalist dogma.

Alexander Goldenweiser ("the philosopher of American anthropology"): "speaking as an American anthropologist I might say: we all partook of functionalism once—before it acquired a capital F"; he cites a passage from an article

---

was a very pleasant and rewarding experience. On one occasion I was present when A. B. Lewis, curator of ethnology at the Field Museum, showed Malinowski the collection from New Guinea in the museum's storerooms; their discussion of their field experiences and of the specimens in the museum's collections was both inspiring and instructive. In 1934 or '35 Malinowski was a guest in our house in Ann Arbor for a few days between lecture engagements. I saw him on a number of occasions in later years. The photograph that serves as frontispiece of *Man and Culture,* edited by Raymond Firth (1957), was taken by me at a meeting at the University of Chicago in 1938.

Because of a brief absence of Robert Redfield from the campus in the summer of 1931, I was the one to greet Radcliffe-Brown when he arrived at the University of Chicago. In 1932 I attended the meeting of the Central States Anthropological Association at the University of Chicago where I heard two of Radcliffe-Brown's most precocious students tell the assembled anthropologists that up to that time, American anthropology had not produced a single scientific study of an Indian tribe. It was not until later that I learned that by "scientific" Radcliffe-Brown meant a nontemporal, nonhistorical, nonevolutinist study. I saw Radcliffe-Brown at a number of meetings during the years when he was at the University of Chicago.

he had written in 1910 and says: "This, I submit, is functionalism" (1940, p. 471). He also said that a careful student would realize, after reading Malinowski, "that Functionalism (with a capital F) is but a will-o'-the-wisp, whereas the more modest functionalism comprised in it . . . differs not at all from the mode of procedure long since adopted by many American ethnologists" (1941, p. 162).

Herskovits declared that "the principle that each element in a culture must be analyzed in terms of its relationship to other aspects of the totality of which it is a part was implicit in all his [Boas'] work" (1953, p. 6). In a review of Mead's *Growing up in New Guinea,* Kroeber said: ". . . we have here, ethnological 'functionalism' of the purest kind from the heart of the Boas school" (1931, p. 248). Kluckhohn found functionalism of a quality surpassing that of Malinowski in Ann Gayton's *Yokuts-Mono Chiefs and Shamans* (1943, n.2, p. 208).

To turn the tables somewhat, Malinowski observed that "Kroeber, in his *Zuni Kin and Clan,* and Lowie in his fieldwork on the Crow Indians and in his book on *Primitive Society,* have very strongly emphasized the functional point of view in reference to kinship" (1930a, p. 20).

Lowie's position is not self-consistent. In his review of *The Andaman Islanders,* by A. R. Brown (who later became Radcliffe-Brown), Lowie remarked "we shall all heartily sympathize with the author's attempt to explain the parts of Andamanese culture not as isolated fragments but as parts of an organic unity" (1923, p. 575); twelve years later, Lowie presented his synoptic picture of Crow Indian culture. But, on the critical side, Lowie later said of Radcliffe-Brown: "This herald of the 'systematic unity' of cultures has not essayed a single integrated cultural picture since his avowedly immature treatise on the Andamanese" (1937, pp. 223–24). Audrey Richards (a

Malinowski student) observed that "Radcliffe-Brown has often bidden us to study and compare 'total social structures' but has never actually described one" (1957, p. 17).

We have already noted Lowie's criticism of Rivers' use of the term "system." On the first page of *Primitive Society* Lowie has a fine statement on the systemic character of Western culture: "So closely are the several departments of civilization knitted together that concentration on any one of them to the exclusion of all others is an impracticable undertaking. Recent events [World War I] have familiarized us with the mutual dependence of apparently disparate branches of culture." But he closes *Primitive Society* with civilization viewed as "a chaotic jumble," a "thing of shreds and patches."

functionalism: prophets and disciples

Both Malinowski and Radcliffe-Brown had more than a little of the prophet in their personalities and their teachings. Both were possessed of charisma; both were bearers of a message, a different doctrine. For many years the ethnological landscape in the United States had been almost an arid wasteland. There were myriads of facts but little meaning; innumerable particulars but very few generalizations. "A detailed study of particulars seemed [to Boas] more rewarding than the building of systems" (Benedict 1943, p. 33). Reflective thought was in disrepute: "to suggest that something is theoretical," Kluckhohn observed in 1939, "is to suggest that it is slightly indecent" (p. 333). Culture was presented as if it were without rhyme or reason. Evolutionism was taboo. Graduate students had no place to go; nothing meaningful to do (see White 1963 and 1966 for a review of Boas' work and influence).

The advent of Malinowski and Radcliffe-Brown, with their philosophy of ethnology, tended to liberate American graduate students from the confines of Boasian eth-

nology. Many students, I am sure, were attracted to functionalism because it was new to them and different; they
were relieved and encouraged to discover that Boasian
ethnology was not the be-all and end-all of nonbiological
anthropology, as they had been led to believe. But much
more than this was involved in their acceptance of functionalism: it gave meaning to social and cultural data; culture was no longer a hodgepodge of disparate and unrelated traits; societies and cultures were living wholes,
composed of interdependent parts, each of which had its
own place and significance in the system as a whole. Functionalism was a key to new insights and understandings.
It was savory and nourishing.

It is difficult to compare the influence of these two
leaders upon American ethnology. Radcliffe-Brown was
on the faculty of a great university in the very heartland of
the United States from 1931 to 1937, where his influence
was direct and personal. Malinowski had visited the
United States in 1926 but did not become a member of the
faculty at Yale University until 1939. He was widely read,
however, and his influence was great.

"As a teacher, Radcliffe-Brown excelled," writes Fortes.
"He warmed to his audience, especially if it was young
. . . [he had] the gift for imparting to students the thrill of
discovery and the desire to join in the task of further research" (Fortes 1956, p. 152 and 1949, p.v).* "Radcliffe-
Brown was a starter and stirrer" said A. P. Elkin (1956,
p. 239). Robert Redfield aptly characterized Radcliffe-
Brown's achievement in the United States as follows: "He

* An interesting footnote on the influence of Radcliffe-Brown's teaching: Linton's correspondence of the period indicates that he deplored
Radcliffe-Brown's considerable influence on younger members of the
profession as a threat to the larger traditional concerns of American anthropology and one which he felt personally obligated to combat"
(Sharp 1968, p. 388).

stirred us up and accelerated intellectual invention and variation among us" (1955, p. ix; see White 1966, pp. 28–51 for a review of Radcliffe-Brown's work and influence).

I believe that Redfield's insight here was both keen and sound. The impact made upon American ethnology by Radcliffe-Brown and Malinowski was much more than the indoctrination of younger anthropologists with a new creed to replace the old one. In a literal sense Malinowski and Radcliffe-Brown "stirred up" the anthropological community; they broke the log-jam, so to speak, and encouraged the consideration of *any* point of view and philosophy in ethnology: as Redfield said, ". . . accelerated intellectual invention and variation among us." Three decades of isolationism * in American ethnology had been terminated at last. Even the monumental Boas was moved.

We have already noted the reasons why students of Boas could not accept "the doctrine of the 'functionalists' " as explained by Leslie Spier: because "every culture . . . [is] a congeries of disconnected traits. . . . functionally unrelated." I believe that Spier's assessment of the rejection of functionalists by Boas and his students is both realistic and accurate. But Boas lived in a terrestrial environment as other men and women did, and though he was sturdy as an oak, as hard as granite, he was not wholly impervious to environmental influences—no more than other men and women are.

In 1930, Boas spoke approvingly of Benedict's attempt to envisage and comprehend cultures as integrated wholes, as we have already noted. In 1932 he could write: "culture is integrated" (Boas, p. 612). In his introduction

* "If he [Boas] left anthropology a science, he also left it somewhat bewildered and isolated," (Kroeber 1952, p. 147).

to Benedict's *Patterns of Culture* (1934), Boas again expresses his approval of "the desire to grasp the meaning of a culture as a whole" (p. xvi). And in *General Anthropology,* (1938a), editor Boas wrote: ". . . the principal problem [of anthropology] . . . [is] that of understanding a culture as a whole" (p. 5). In his chapter, "Methods of Research," he said "it seems most desirable and worth while to understand each culture as a whole." (p. 680). His conversion was complete.

It is interesting to consider the chronology of this about-face. If my reckoning is correct, Boas was seventy-two years old when he first spoke approvingly of conceiving of cultures as integrated wholes. He was eighty years old when he declared that "the principal problem of anthropology" was the "understanding of a culture as a whole." The rising tide of conceiving cultures as integrated wholes—from Herbert Spencer, through the Fabian Socialists, and the work of Durkheim, to Benedict, the value studies, and the functionalists—eventually reached and embraced Franz Boas. Had his life ended with the traditional "three score and ten," he would never have attained this enlightenment.

malinowski and radcliffe-brown compared

We find little in the writings of Malinowski that deals with systems. As a matter of fact, despite his insights, his vivid and sometimes dramatic expositions, I cannot help but feel that Malinowski was not a thoroughgoing scientist and, moreover, I believe that he would have agreed with me here. I believe that he felt that some of his intuitions and comprehensions lay outside the boundaries of rigorous science. He was an artist in the sense that his great compatriot—also Anglicized—Joseph Conrad was. The desire to understand "the native . . . his outlook on things, his *Weltanschauung,* the breath of life and reality which he breathes and by which he lives. . . . the possibility of seeing life and the world . . . peculiar to each culture, that has always charmed me most, and inspired me with real desire to penetrate other cultures." (1922, p. 517) somewhat resembles Conrad's desire to plumb the depths of Lord Jim's soul. Scientist or not, Malinowski was certainly not a culturologist, although he uses phrases on occasion that are compatible with culturological theory. His conception of functionalism comes closer to the older concept of social organism than it does to a culturological conception of systems.

Radcliffe-Brown comes much closer to science than does Malinowski, in my opinion. He defined culture in such a way as to put it outside the scope of scientific study, but much of his work is culturological in nature, i.e., explanation of cultural (he calls them social) phenomena in cultural (social) terms rather than in terms of psychology (see White 1969, n., p. 98, and White 1966, pp. 42–44).

Radcliffe-Brown implicitly considers culture (as I use this term) as a whole, as a system. But in his writings he tends to limit himself to kinship systems, social or political systems; he does not embrace culture as a whole. Especially does he disregard, except perhaps for incidental references, technology and mode of subsistence. And nowhere does he consider a cultural system in terms of its component vectors.

review

Looking back over the past century—from Spencer's "A Society is an Organism" to the present day—we observe a groping, a tropismatic trend toward the concept of a cultural system with its interdependent working parts, its vectors. We observe a trend toward making explicit the proposition that the behavior of the system as a whole is the synthesis of its component vectors in terms of their respective magnitudes. The concept of social organism was the progenitor of the concept of cultural system. As we have seen, there has been considerable opposition to the conception of organic cultural wholes, especially in the United States: Boas, Benedict, Spier, and Lowie to a certain extent. We have traced the progress of Benedict from "the superstition" of organic unity to psychological types, configurations, and then patterns of culture. Eventually, Boas himself was caught up in the trend that he then unequivocally endorsed.

The unity (wholeness) of cultures was made explicit by Rivers in 1922, and he was followed by the functionalists who, in the Radcliffe-Brown group, added the concept of system and *the behavior of systems,* to the conception of organic unity. But no one, as far as I know, had produced a study of cultural systems that sets forth each structure as a whole in terms of all its vectors, shows how these vectors behave as individual vectors, how they interact with one another, and, finally, how the system as a whole behaves as an expression of the synthesis of the behavior of its component vectors in terms of their respective magnitudes. We have no studies at all of nations as cultural systems, and very few, if any, such studies of tribes.

The urgent need of today is a rigorous scientific study of nations as cultural systems, delineating their various vectors, technological, sociological, and ideological, and showing how and to what extent each contributes to the synthesis that is the behavior of the nation as a whole.

some reflections upon and implications of this essay

MANY reflections and implications are raised; we shall consider only a few. First of all, the concept of cultural systems changes radically some of our previous conceptions of the relationship between culture—a suprabiological order of phenomena—and the human species. We no longer think of culture as designed to serve the needs of man; culture goes its own way in accordance with laws of its own. Man lives within the embrace of cultural systems, and enjoys or suffers whatever they mete out to him.

Many individuals in a certain stratum of society in the United States have felt—rather than thought—that there are some absolutes in their society and culture, something like the velocity of light in physical theory, or the North Star in navigation; something to which everything else can be referred and by which everything can be evaluated. The Constitution provides us with one example. The conception of Justice (with a capital J) that abides with us, never changing, is another expression of this attitude. I do not know how to distinguish these individuals as a class with any degree of precision, but I would say that they tend to belong to the middle, or upper-middle, class, have college educations, and like to think of themselves as "liberals." I was brought up in this tradition; but my prolonged and earnest concern with cultural systems has changed my outlook in this respect.

We have thought (or felt) that however the Ship of State might flounder, get off course, there was always "The Constitution," standing steadfast as a beacon to bring the mariner back upon his true course. But what does the Constitution say and mean? It says and means whatever the United States Supreme Court decides it says and means. It is not the rock upon which our nation was built and upon which it rests. It is a weather vane that shows which way the winds of society and culture are blowing, a register of social and cultural change.

In the first place, the Constitution has been changed or enlarged by twenty-six amendments, and there are more to come. The decisions of the Supreme Court—the chief justice and the eight associate justices—are not always, or even frequently, unanimous; some are five to four decisions. Yet, with all its amendments and the sharply divided decisions of the Supreme Court, many individuals in the class that I have tried to identify feel that "*the* meaning, the *real* meaning" of the Constitution is being revealed. An understanding of the operation of vectors in our cultural system gives us a more realistic appreciation of the judicial process. We see now that the Supreme Court is an area in which various vectors of our cultural system come together, each one exerting itself in terms of its magnitude (the ability to influence decisions), and eventually forming a synthesis which constitutes the Court's "decision." In anthropomorphic terms, "the nation can make any decision that it wants to make." The middle-class liberal is distressed by this view. No longer does he have the Constitution standing firm like a sturdy oak, guaranteeing the liberties of the citizenry. Instead, he finds himself buffeted about by the winds of social, political, and economic change, winds that often seem to him capricious and unjust. What is unconstitutional today may be accepted tomorrow. The federal income tax law of 1894 was declared unconstitutional; it became constitutional, however, in 1913. The Constitution may be obliged, by the ebb and flow of social forces, by powerful pressure groups, to repudiate its own decisions. The about-face with regard to the manufacture, transportation, and sale of intoxicating liquors is a good example.

A temperance movement got under way in the United States during the first decade of the nineteenth century. A Prohibition party nominated its first candidate for President in 1872. Two years later the Women's Christian Temperance Union was founded. The Anti-Saloon League was organized in 1893 and quickly became one of the most powerful pressure groups in America. Many church groups and some industrialists supported the temperance movement. In 1914 a prohibition amendment received a majority in the House of Representatives. The Eighteenth Amendment, prohibiting the manufacture, sale, or transportation of intoxicating liquors, was proposed by Congress in 1917; it was ratified in 1919. "There followed a period of unparalleled illegal drinking (often of inferior and dangerous beverages) and lawbreaking" (*The Columbia Encyclopedia,* 3d ed., s.v. "prohibition"). The Congress, responding to social pressures, proposed the Twenty-first Amendment in February of 1933; it was ratified in December of the same year. Then, it was no longer illegal to manufacture, sell, transport—or drink—intoxicating liquors.

Actually, some of the founding fathers clearly recognized that the Constitution was a provisional instrument of government. Thomas Jefferson said that one should not regard it as the Ark of the Covenant, that as times change so should our institutions change. "Let us provide for its [the Constitutions's] revision at stated times," said Jefferson (as quoted by Harry Elmer Barnes 1926, p. 334). But the folklore of democracy persists in presenting the

Constitution as the Ark of the Covenant (the chest containing the two stone tablets inscribed with the Ten Commandments).

As with the Constitution, so with Justice. All human societies have been concerned with justice, with good and evil, and with fair treatment for all. To many members of the class I have tried to characterize (but have been unable to name), Justice, with a capital J, is something inherent in the structure of the cosmos and the nature of man; it is eternal and unchanging. Justice, they feel, is the goal of both custom and the courts. Values are absolute ("abortion is murder"; "if something is wrong it's wrong; if it is right it's right"). And, according to this view, the legal and judicial system can and will see that Justice is done. This view is, however, a naive one.

An understanding of the vectors—the "interests," the pressure groups—that comprise cultural systems reveals the realities of "justice," if not the ideal. What is one man's justice is another man's tyranny and exploitation. Not a few clergymen in the United States during the first half of the nineteenth century found justice in chattel slavery—and appealed to the Bible to justify their attitude. Lynching, assassination, dueling, prisons, capital punishment, almshouses, child labor, prostitution, usury, etc., have been justified at one time or another. One nation's traitor may be another nation's hero. Persons of wealth and political influence may go free where the common man would go to prison. Justice and injustice may be but two sides of a synthesis effected by vectors, by pressure groups, and by class structure, within a cultural system.

Our system for the administration of justice is ideally structured to accommodate diverse and conflicting vectors. Superficially, a trial resembles the physicist who determines the specific gravity of a substance; the trial determines guilt and non-guilt. But here the resemblance stops: the trial is not conducted by a unified body that observes, weighs, and measures. On the contrary, it is divided against itself: one part strives for conviction; the other for acquittal. The object of each side is not to mete out justice but to win. Within the wide limits of the law, almost any device may be employed by the attorneys on each side to win their case. If the defense calls in a psychiatrist to prove that his client was insane at the time he committed homicide, the prosecution can call in a psychiatrist to prove that the accused was perfectly capable of distinguishing "right" from "wrong" and therefore was sane. In food and drug litigation each side may produce physicians and pharmacologists to support its case; the trial takes on the aspect of a baseball game, each side with its own coach.

Admittedly, of course, the analogy between determining the specific gravity of a substance and determining the guilt of one accused of a certain act *is* an analogy. There might be no question of fact: reliable eye witnesses saw Mr. X shoot and kill Mr. Y. But the question Was Mr. X justified in killing Mr. Y? may be legally pertinent to the trial. There have been instances in our history where a husband who killed his wife's lover was considered to be justified in doing so. The law distinguishes between voluntary and involuntary manslaughter. Careful observation and measurement may be sufficient in physics; moral judgment must be applied in many instances in the administration of justice.

But our initial statement that the legal/judicial system provides almost innumerable opportunities for vectors to apply pressure to the judicial process remains valid: the most powerful pressure group has the best chance of success.

The object of each side in a trial, the prosecution and the defense, is not to do justice but to win. In this respect the trial resembles a baseball game. Within the wide limits of the law, the lawyers on both sides may resort to cunning, misrepresentation, distortion, innuendo, praise, or ridicule. Their summations before the jury may be exercises in histrionics designed to sway the jurors one way or another. The jurors are not always impartial or objective: "Evidence! Just look at his eyes!"

If the person on trial is of sufficient prominence to be quoted by the news media, and is found "guilty as charged," he invariably calls the trial "a gross miscarriage of justice" (i.e., he did not win). But if the verdict is "not guilty," he piously remarks that "his faith in the essential justice of the American judicial system has been vindicated and sustained" (i.e., he won).

If the accused is found guilty by the jury, the defense can move for a mistrial or retrial on some technicality: that the accused was not properly informed of his rights when he was arrested; or that evidence used to convict him was obtained illegally; or that the judge erred in his instructions to the jury. If the accused is found guilty he can appeal his case to a higher court, providing he can afford attorney fees. This appeal gives interest groups another opportunity to influence a decision. One court can overrule another. A case can ascend the judicial ladder from court to court until it reaches the Supreme Court. Here, the analogy with a baseball game will not serve: if a player is called out at first, he is out at first; if team A does not win the pennant, team A does not win the pennant.

If a verdict of guilty is sustained, the convicted person may be released on probation or he may be sent to prison. "Plea bargaining" may allow a person charged with several offenses to have all remaining charges dismissed after he has pleaded "guilty" or "no contest" to one of them. A person in a high place may go free where a common citizen would go to prison. If a person receives a sentence of life imprisonment, or of death in a gas chamber, his sentence may be commuted by the governor of a state or by the president of the United States. In a "democracy," the largest and most powerful vector, or pressure group, is that of Public Opinion: Justice becomes whatever the cultural system decides is justice. And, according to the mythology of Democracy, where the People are sovereign, there can be no appeal from their verdict.

It is my opinion, as an ethnographer of many years, that the common people, the working classes, in the United States view justice more realistically than do the "middle classes," the intellectuals and liberals, with their idealism, genuine or spurious.

the morality of politicians

It is widely believed by voters in the United States that politicians—in and out of office—are a venal lot. A cry raised before any major election calls upon the voters to "turn the rascals [the office holders] out," and, of course, put honest men and women in their place. Whether or not the calling of politician tends to attract the venal to its ranks is a question that we must leave unanswered simply because we do not know how to substantiate such a charge. But we can throw some light on this situation.

A person running for office declares his purposes and desires and solemnly promises to carry them out if and when he is elected. But should he be elected he discovers, if he does not know already, that he must reckon with many powerful factors—the influence of his colleagues, the pressures of numerous interest groups, the possibility of bribes or threats, and so on. He may be induced to go beyond the law; in a situation of litigation he may be pushed to the point of perjury. He is caught up in a maelstrom of vectors, pushed here and there by forces outside himself and beyond his control. Broken are his pre-election pledges; his promises become "campaign oratory" (Wendell Willkie). The arena of competing vectors can deal ruthlessly with an honest man.

harmony of parts

In order to function effectively and, in the last analysis, to survive, a system must realize a synthesis among its several parts—a working harmony among them—and it must subordinate part to whole.

We have already spoken of the principle of the separation of powers in the structure of the government of the United States and the reason therefor. Obstacles to harmony and integration were built into the American system. But freedom for autonomous action of parts has gone far beyond the three segments: executive, legislative, and judicial. Virtually anyone, any citizen who enjoys prestige and popularity, can speak out freely and in accents of authority to tell the nation what it should or should not do. Senators, congressmen, big bankers, corporation executives, clergymen, editors, columnists, generals and admirals, physicists, economists, biologists, labor unions, farmers' organizations, etc., can speak out, appeal to "the American people," for or against any action taken by the President, the Congress, or the Supreme Court. Among the courts, the extent to which one court can overrule another is astonishing. Any one of the hundreds of congressmen or of the one hundred United States senators has the right to initiate legislation in any field and for any purpose without regard to any over-all plan; the Congress has none. The nation runs its affairs like a New England town meeting of colonial days. This has been greatly admired and praised as "the essence of Democracy." This it may be, but it makes the operation of a large nation exceedingly ineffectual. The nation frequently finds itself a congeries of factions, one pitted against another (the Vietnam war, the forcible bussing of school children).

I must now make a few points perfectly clear. I am not arguing or even suggesting that individuals or organizations should not express themselves freely. On the contrary, such expression is essential to the health of a cultural system and its ability to behave effectively. The point I wish to make is that syntheses of diverse parts and interests should not be made at the top of the system but at lower levels (when I say "should" here it is with the qualification "if the system is to function effectively"). For maximum effectiveness—in an ideal system—syntheses should be effected in all areas and at all levels leading to the top of the system. Thus, agriculture, manufacturing, labor, and other major vectors should achieve syntheses within themselves. This would be followed by a synthesis of the major vectors. *Then* the nation, the system as a whole, would have its course of action clearly indicated.

In the United States, however, all issues are thrown out into the national arena there to be kicked about or defended by anyone who cares to take part.

Cultural evolution has not yet produced a highly developed national system. The monolithic, one-party nations give the appearance of having reached the stage where syntheses are made at the top. But it is widely claimed that this is achieved at the expense of free expression and synthesis on lower levels.

subordination of part to whole

In any normal or "healthy" system, component parts are subordinated to whole. But there are imperfect systems in which autonomy of a part may overcome subordination. When this happens the system suffers.

Strikes afford an example of failure of a system to subordinate part to whole. Indeed, a strike by a very small portion of the work force of the country—locomotive engineers, longshoremen, coal miners, truckers, nurses, municipal workers—can cripple or paralyze large segments of the nation. A strike by one group, one that delivers parts, for example, may bring an entire manufacturing process to a standstill. The assertion of autonomy of a part (i.e., a strike) by its very nature ignores the general welfare, and in addition to preventing other parts from performing their respective functions, it may bring about a menace to public health by allowing garbage to accumulate, or by dumping millions of gallons of raw sewage into a bay or river, or by depriving a community of fire protection or hospital care.

Please note that I am not passing moral judgments here. The question of the justification of a strike is not relevant to our discussion. Strikes take place; they have causes and consequences. I am concerned here only with the problem of the relationship of part to whole in cultural systems; clarification rather than justification or condemnation is our goal. The problem of strikes, the disruption of process, and the waste of performance or output is compounded by the fact that the nation's work force does not all strike at once, as the cost of living increases. Far from this, all workers in a single industry—the transportation workers, for example—do not strike at one time. One strike follows another endlessly; there is hardly a time when there are not at least a few strikes in progress. The cost to the nation in convenience is great, the loss of output is enormous.

This problem has its history. The struggle of wage labor for the right to form unions, first of all; the right to strike, to bargain collectively—has put labor in a position of great power in our national cultural system. These gains of labor have been incorporated into the "democratic way of life" to the preservation of which all components of the system are dedicated. Considerable time has passed since federal troops, the national guard, or deputized police have been used to break strikes. Until the problem of the relationship between the vectors segments of labor and the nation as a whole can be solved, the nation will be vulnerable to paralyzing strikes, its stability will be impaired, and its ability to function will be effectively weakened.

Government by a dictator, backed by force, may prevent strikes, but such a system is, by its very nature, unstable. How the problem will be solved, if indeed it can be solved in a "free society," is not clear at present. The indications are, however, that it may be solved and the would-be strikers brought back into harmony with the nation as a whole by some form of "compulsory arbitration" that, however, must be acceptable to the strikers. How *compulsory* arbitration can be made acceptable is the question to be answered.

subordination of big business
to the national cultural system

At the other end of the spectrum are the great corporations and the mighty banks. We must be careful to make an important distinction here. The vectors composing a cultural system will be of unequal strengths and magnitudes; one or a very few will be the strongest vectors in the system. And in nations in modern western culture, the giant corporations and banks may constitute the most powerful vector or vectors in the national cultural system. But the point is not merely one of the strength of the corporate or banking vectors, but whether, strong as they are, they are well integrated into the system; whether they, as part or parts, are subordinated to the system as a whole.

In 1913 Woodrow Wilson observed that "the government of the United States . . . is a foster-child of the special interests. . . . the big bankers, the big manufacturers, the big masters of commerce, the heads of railroad corporations and of steamship corporations. . . . [The government] is not allowed to have a will of its own" (pp. 57–58).

In 1932, Adolf A. Berle and Gardiner C. Means asserted that the concentration of economic power in the great corporations of that day enabled them to "compete on equal terms with the modern state." Going further, they suggested that "the future may see the economic organism, now typified by the corporation, not only on an equal plane with the state, but possibly even superseding it as the dominant form of social organization" (p. 357).

The State, as the mechanism of integration of the cultural system that is the United States, has made many efforts—the antitrust legislation is perhaps the most significant—to bring corporations, powerful though they be, to a position of a *part* subordinated to the *whole*. But Professor Andrew Hacker has recently asserted that "our ideology permits us to rest happy in the thought that the Anti-Trust Division of the Justice Department could, if it so desires, 'break up' General Dynamics or International Business Machines into congeries of separate companies. The fact of power, however, is that this has not, cannot, and will not be done *because government is weaker than the corporate institutions purportedly subordinate to it,"* (1964, p. 11; emphasis added).

The cultural system that is the United States has evolved considerably during the past century; it has gone a long way from the days of the tycoons of industry and the finance of laissez faire of the nineteenth century—Cornelius Vanderbilt, Colis P. Huntington, J. P. Morgan, et al. This fact might encourage the belief that within the next half-century the nation will succeed in subordinating its most powerful parts to the harmony of the whole. But how it will be done—if it can be done—remains to be seen. Can the process of integration of parts keep pace with—or overcome—the increase in size?

occupational organization and representation

As we have noted, the government of the United States was organized on a territorial, or areal, basis, and the citizenry is represented by officials elected by the voters of these various segments: states, congressional districts, counties, cities, wards, etc. And we have raised the question of representation: How can a congressman, for example, elected by the voters in a congressional district, represent the many, and sometimes conflicting, interests in his district—tenants and landlords, employers and employees, loan companies and borrowers, farmers and manufacturers, or those in medicine, education, science, the fine arts, etc.? We have noted, also, that society in the United States is, in actuality, organized along occupational lines (farmers, miners, engineers, physicians, merchants, teachers) and special interest groups (women, the elderly, ethnic minorities, consumers, giant corporations, etc.). Our discussion of lobbying has shown that it is these sectors of society and the economy that are in actuality represented vis-à-vis government by their respective lobbyists. The question arises, therefore, why should not the governmental structure of the nation, its system of representation of interest groups, be organized in harmony with actualities rather than in terms of unrealistic geographic divisions?

The geographic basis of organization and representation made some sense in the days of the founding fathers when the nation was predominantly rural and agricultural. But even then there were powerful mercantile, manufacturing, financial, shipping, etc., interests. With the evolution of American culture the geographic basis of representation has become increasingly unrealistic and may now be considered obsolete.

Our essay on cultural systems invites speculation as well as reflection. Are we moving in the direction of representation by interest group rather than by territorial segment? This question is not a new one, by any means. Over eighty years ago the great French sociologist-culturologist Émile Durkheim, who was possessed of great foresight as well as insight and understanding, wrote: "a day will come when our whole social and political organization will have a base exclusively, or almost exclusively, occupational" (1960, [1893] p. 190).

American society and culture are undergoing revolutionary change. They have gone a long way from laissez faire to welfare. Human rights are being elevated above property rights in many sectors. The principle that human beings have rights *as human beings*—rights to medical care, to a decent standard of living—is becoming established. This is in marked contrast with American culture of the nineteenth century when strikes were punished as "criminal conspiracies," when thousands of poor people were herded into the degradation and dehumanization of almshouses, when tycoons of industry and finance (the "robber barons") could ride roughshod over the economy and its human casualties ("The public be damned").

The actualities of today are representation of interest groups by extralegal or quasi-legal lobbyists. Will the day come, as Durkheim predicted, when such representation will become de jure as well as de facto? Our social revolution is still in progress and is accelerating.

In this connection we recall that a complete and comprehensive plan for the reorganization of American society upon an occupational basis was worked out by the great American socialist Daniel De Leon (1852–1914), considered by Lenin "the greatest of modern Socialists—the only one who has added anything to Socialist thought since Marx" (Raisky 1932, p. 47; see also Jászi 1934 pp. 205–6). De Leon worked out a plan of Industrial Unionism that was to become the form of government after the industrial workers triumphed and instituted production for use rather than for profit.

We recall, also, the Syndicalist movement in France and some Latin countries in the nineteenth century. It held that the trade union was to become the essential unit of production and of government. In the United States syndicalism found expression in the Industrial Workers of the World, which flourished in the early years of the twentieth century. Also, we must take note of Guild Socialism of England, which envisaged a system of industrial self-government through national worker-controlled guilds.

This exceedingly brief historical sketch reveals cultural tropisms on a wide front since 1800, tropisms groping toward an occupational organization of society.

tribe and nation as cultural systems

In the process of the evolution of culture, the tribe and the nation are the two major forms of cultural systems; as a matter of fact, they are the only significant cultural systems in human history. They are the most compact, the best integrated, the most viable and durable social organisms that cultural evolution has produced. The tribe, organized upon the basis of kinship and characterized by liberty, equality, and fraternity, has been the cultural system that has been most congenial to the biological nature of the talking primate that has ever existed. Its connective tissue was tough and strong; its structure well adapted to the exploitation of natural resources and to survival in an arena of ruthless competition. In short, it possessed all the attributes that are necessary to form and to preserve a system, a cultural system.

The institutions of preliterate tribal society were rendered obsolete by the Agricultural Revolution, a furnace in which a new type of cultural system was wrought and welded together: the nation-state. Tribalism did not give up without a struggle, however, and one sees today in the formation of new nations in Black Africa how tribe and nation are struggling for supremacy.

Both tribe and nation are systems that weld themselves and preserve themselves by the most powerful of bonds: tribal loyalty and national patriotism. All civil societies, all nations, have suffered internal conflicts: the insurrection of the serfs, slaves, peasants, and proletariat. But few, if any, have been destroyed by civil wars. In recent centuries we have witnessed the growth of an international proletarian movement. Leaders of the Second Socialist International, meeting in Switzerland in the spring of 1914, pledged themselves, and urged their followers, to stand fast in the war that was then imminent, to transform a capitalist war among nations into an international proletarian war for the emancipation of the working class. But when the cannons began to roar and the smell of gunpowder spread across the land, the working class of each nation answered the call of the Fatherland, the Mother Country. National solidarity was proven stronger than international working-class solidarity.

And so it was with World War II. Many "liberals" saw in this war an opportunity for "the masses to rise up and throw off the yoke of dictatorship," imperialism, and economic exploitation and subjugation. But they had not reckoned realistically with the tough integument of patriotism that binds together the cultural system of nations with the strongest bonds known to modern man. The men and women of Communist and Fascist dictatorships, oriental empires, and capitalist nations alike stood fast and died by the millions for the Fatherland, the Mother Country.

National sovereignty and patriotism go hand in hand; each nourishes and sustains the other. In former times they contributed greatly to the survival of nations; they were means of mobilizing all the resources of a nation to succeed in the ruthless struggle among nations for power and even for their very existence. This is how cultural systems preserve themselves.

Today, however, national sovereignty constitutes the greatest nontechnological threat, not only to the existence of nations as autonomous and sovereign cultural systems, but to the very existence of culture and man himself. The advent of the hydrogen bomb and intercontinental missiles have signaled the end of global wars. This is fully realized by many men and women—some of them heads of states—in every nation capable of nuclear war, and in many nations that can only be passive victims of such a holocaust. But are nations—cultural systems—capable of preventing such a war? People, human beings, may have hope and faith, but there is very little hard evidence that *nations* will—or even *can*—move against their very nature and sacrifice sovereignty for survival.

As we have seen, cultural systems are incapable of behavior that can be called intelligent; they are limited to reflexes and tropisms. The habits of centuries are powerful. Threats to national sovereignty must be repulsed; national honor must be upheld. Threat is countered with threat. Disarmament talks are held while armaments are piled and stockpiled in vast amounts to insure that they will never be used: the bow and arrow, the crossbow, cannon, bombs, and rockets have all had their day as "deterrents" in a series of wars that never ends. This is the sort of intelligence that marks the "mind" of nations. Recently a great state ordered a global alert for all of its military forces. Had another great power met this gesture with one of its own, and had the marionette defenders of national sovereignty and honor raised their voices in hot anger and defiance, the shroud of death might have been spread over worldwide radioactive rubble.

can the saurian state survive?

"Can the saurian state survive?" is the question of the day. Nations go from crisis to crisis—crises that they can neither comprehend nor control. Monetary crises and inflation are to the national mind like awesome solar eclipses and vengeful hurricanes were to the dark mind of the savage: powerful, ominous, and incomprehensible—except to shamans and augurs.

Like the dinosaurs of the Mesozoic, the great nations of today have huge bodies but rudimentary brains. Their very hugeness poses problems: how are they to hold their diverse parts together—the proliferating technology, the minorities, the conflicting classes, the highly diversified economy, the mysterious bloodstream of gold that defies understanding and control. Even in times of peace they are finding it more and more difficult to solve the least of their problems.

The hegemony of the dinosaurs endured for millions of years. They became extinct, not because of the limitations of their reptilian brains, for their tropisms and reflexes served them well, but because cataclysmic convulsions of the earth radically changed their habitat in temperature, climate, and food supply. The threats facing the modern nation are, however, principally of their own making. Increase in population has become a dire threat largely because advances in medical technology have saved millions who might otherwise have died of plagues. Food-producing technology has increased the world's food supply, which permits millions to exist who otherwise would have died of starvation or malnutrition (no moral judgments are being made here at all; we merely call attention to the sequence of cause and effect). The earth's atmosphere and the waters of the earth are being polluted at an ever-increasing rate, rapidly making our planet uninhabitable. At least, the dimunitive brain of the saurians cannot be blamed for the deleterious change in their habitats.

We wish to examine threats to the survival of the saurian nations of today arising from the nature of the cultural systems themselves. For a system to persist it must be able to do certain things. First of all, it must maintain the energy input; if the amount of energy available to its use is diminished the system will shrink and eventually disintegrate. Second, it must maintain a certain degree of cohesion, otherwise it will fall apart. As we have noted earlier, the cohesiveness of a system diminishes as its size increases, other factors being constant; there is a limit to the size of a drop of water or mercury; an ocean liner would break up of its own size and weight upon reaching a certain point. The process of segmentation makes possible increases in size of a system, be it physical, biological, or cultural. Theoretically, at least, a single sociocultural organization embracing the whole earth and the entire human race is a possibility; but the chances of this goal—complete surrender of national sovereignty—being reached before pollution makes the planet uninhabitable or thermonuclear war terminates the existence of culture, are not promising as the situation looks today. As culture evolves the cultural systems that are nations become much more complex. The velocity of the process of evolution is greater in the cultural than the biological field. Theoretically, cultural evolution should be able to produce the equivalent of the mammalian brain—even the talking-primate brain—in much less time than was required to produce it by biological evolution. But the question is, What is the likelihood that our culture will produce such a mechanism of integration of parts and regulation of behavior before it is overcome by pollution or global warfare? From where we stand today, the chances of this happening do not appear to be good.

Technology has been the great prime mover and the architect of cultural systems, by and large, throughout the long course of cultural development. The technology of the present day is astonishing in its high degree of development, its ingenuity, its power and momentum. Will it not be sufficient to create a sociopolitical system that can not only contain the mighty forces of technology but can insure progressive cultural development? This is an inviting thought: if we can put a man on the moon and explore the planets with unmanned spacecraft can we not construct an enduring, worldwide cultural system? But, "We can put a man on the moon, but we cannot make our city streets safe for its citizens at night." More significant than this, however, is the fact that, in order for a creative technology to construct a world state, national sovereignities will have to be dismantled. We see no signs whatever of the abolition of national sovereignty, whether ultimately or in the near future: "I'd rather be dead than Red." "The United States must be a world power second to none." "Deutschland über alles." Furthermore, the highest development of technology today is to be found in the technology of war, the technology of destruction. And this technology is in the hands of sovereign nations.

There are those who seek reassurance in the reasoning that says, "we've always managed in the past, we've surmounted great obstacles and survived great dangers, and we'll manage to do so in the future." But this tends to overlook the careers of great cultural systems of the past—Sumeria, Hittites, Babylonia, Egypt, Rome, the Maya. Empires tend to be ephemeral. Reflexes and tropisms have guided cultural systems in the past, but are they—will they be—sufficient to create and guide a stage of political evolution beyond that of the sovereign state, i.e., a global system? Again we are confronted by the fact that the cultures of the modern world are locked in by the cultural systems of sovereign states, and until and unless they can be "unlocked"—emancipated from the sacred bonds of national sovereignty—the prospects for the future of civilization are rather grim. The saurian states of today, armed to the teeth and jealous of their rights, their power, and their honor, may well "contain the seeds of their own destruction."

The doctrine of cultural determinism is scientifically sound and pedagogically illuminating. The concepts of culture and cultural systems are the two basic concepts in the science of culture. Adherence to the principle of cause and effect—and rejection of the sweet, soothing teats of free will and anthropocentrism—require courage and even ruthlessness. We can understand the cry of anguish of C. Judson Herrick, a very distinguished neurologist of his day, when confronted by the doctrines of the culturologist: they "lead to nihilism that would paralyze all man's efforts to improve his condition. . . . [to] a dismal fatalism and . . . a confession of defeat" (1956, p. 196). I admit that the doctrines of culturology can be depressing. But what revolution in science has brought comfort to the human ego—the Copernican, which denied to the earth, man's habitat, a central place in the cosmos, the Darwinian, which stripped man of his celestial attributes and placed him upon the earth as a cousin of the apes?

> I love truth. I believe that mankind needs it, but certainly it has still more need of the illusion which flatters

it, consoles it and gives it infinite hopes. Without illusion, it would perish of despair and ennui (Anatole France).

But if science is feared, it is above all because it cannot give us happiness. Of course it cannot. We may even ask whether the beast does not suffer less than man. But can we regret that earthly paradise where man brute-like was really immortal in knowing not that he must die? When we have tasted the apple, no suffering can make us forget its savor. We always come back to it. Could it be otherwise? As well ask if one who has seen and is blind will not long for the lights. Man, then, can not be happy through science, but today he can much less be happy without it (Henri Poincaré 1913, p. 206).

BIBLIOGRAPHY

Aberle, David F., Urie Bronfenbrenner, Eckhard H. Hess, Daniel R. Miller, David M. Schneider, and James N. Spuhler. 1963. "The Incest Taboo and the Mating Patterns of Animals." *American Anthropologist* 65:253–65.

Addams, Jane. 1960. *A Centennial Reader.* (A collection of essays, addresses, etc., over a long period of time.) New York: Macmillan.

Ayres, Eugene and Charles A. Scarlott. 1952. *Energy Resources: The Wealth of the World.* New York: McGraw-Hill.

Barnes, Harry E. 1925. "Representative Biological Theories of Society." *Sociological Review* 17:120–30, 182–94, 194, 300.

——. 1926. *History and Social Intelligence.* New York: Knopf.

Beals, Ralph L. and Harry Hoijer. 1953. *An Introduction to Anthropology.* New York: Macmillan.

Benedict, Ruth. 1923. "The Guardian Spirit in North America." *Memoir 23: American Anthropological Association.*

——. 1930. "Psychological Types in the Cultures of the Southwest." *Proceedings of the 23d International Congress of Americanists,* New York, 1928. Reprinted in *Readings in Social Psychology,* publication of the Society for the Study of Social Issues. New York: Henry Holt for the Society.

——. 1932. "Configurations of Culture in North America." *American Anthropologist* 34:1–27.

——. 1934. *Patterns of Culture.* Boston: Houghton Mifflin. Sentry ed., 1961, containing a new preface by Margaret Mead and an introduction by Franz Boas.

——. 1943. "Franz Boas as an Ethnologist." In Franz Boas: 1858–1942. *Memoir 61: American Anthropological Association.*

Berle, Adolf A. 1965. *The American Economic Republic.* New York: Harcourt, Brace, and World.

Berle, Adolf A. and Gardiner C. Means. 1932. *The Modern Corporation and Private Property.* New York: Macmillan.

Bidney, David. 1954. Review of *Culture: A Critical Review of Concepts and Definitions,* by A. L. Kroeber and Clyde Kluckhohn. *American Journal of Sociology* 59:488–89.

Boas, Franz. 1896. "The Limitations of the Comparative Method of Anthropology." *Science*, n.s., 4:901–8. Reprinted in Boas, *Race, Language and Culture*, 1940.

———. 1897. "The Social Organization and Secret Societies of the Kwakiutl Indians." Report of the U.S. National Museum for 1895, pp. 660–64. Washington. Reproduced with slight modifications in *Race, Language and Culture*, 1940.

———. 1898a. "The Mythology of the Bella Coola Indians." *Memoirs: American Museum of Natural History*, vol. 2. Publications of the Jesup North Pacific Expedition (vol. 1, edited by Franz Boas). New York.

———. 1898b. "Operations of the [Jesup North Pacific] Expedition in 1897." Publications of the Jesup North Pacific Expedition, 1:1–18. New York.

———. 1924. "Evolution or Diffusion?" *American Anthropologist* 26:340–44. Reprinted in Boas, *Race, Language and Culture*, 1940.

———. 1928. *Anthropology and Modern Life*. New York: Norton.

———. 1930. "Anthropology." *Encyclopedia of the Social Sciences*, vol. 2.

———. 1932. "The Aims of Anthropological Research." Address of the president of the *American Association for the Advancement of Science* 76:605–13.

———. 1938a. *Introduction to General Anthropology*. Franz Boas, ed. Boston, New York: D. C. Heath.

———. 1938b. "Methods of Research." In *Introduction to General Anthropology*. Franz Boas, ed.

———. 1940. *Race, Language and Culture*. New York: Macmillan.

Bohannan, Paul. 1966. Introduction to a new edition of *Houses and House-Life of the American Aborigines*, by Lewis H. Morgan. Chicago: University of Chicago Press.

Bryce, James. 1910. [1888] *The American Commonwealth*, 2 vols. Rev. ed. New York: Macmillan.

Cohen, Yehudi, ed. 1968. *Man in Adaptation: The Cultural Present*. Chicago: Aldine.

Conant, James Bryant. 1951. "A Skeptical Chemist Looks into the Crystal Ball." *Chemical and Engineering News*, vol. 29.

Congressional Quarterly Service. 1968. *Legislators and the Lobbyists*. Washington, D.C.

Conrad, Joseph. 1912. "A Familiar Preface." In *A Personal Record.* Garden City, New York: Doubleday.

Dangerfield, George. 1948. Review of *The Reign of Queen Victoria,* by Hector Bolitho. *Saturday Review of Literature* 31:18.

Daniel, Glyn E. 1950. *A Hundred Years of Archaeology.* London: Duckworth.

Deakin, James. 1966. *The Lobbyists.* Washington, D.C.: Public Affairs Press.

De Laguna, Frederica. 1968. Presidential Address. *American Anthropologist* 70:469–76.

Durkheim, Émile. 1938. [1895] *The Rules of Sociological Method.* Trans. Sarah A. Solovay and John H. Mueller, ed. George E. G. Catlin. Chicago: University of Chicago Press.

———. 1947. [1912] *The Elementary Forms of the Religious Life.* Glencoe, Ill.: The Free Press.

———. 1951. [1897] *Suicide.* Trans. John A. Spaulding and George Simpson. Glencoe, Ill.: The Free Press.

———. 1953. [1898] *Sociology and Philosophy.* Trans. D. F. Pocock. Glencoe, Ill.: The Free Press.

———. 1960. [1893] *The Division of Labor in Society.* Glencoe, Ill.: The Free Press.

Einstein, Albert. 1934. *The World As I See It.* New York: McLeod.

Elkin, A. P. 1956. "A. R. Radcliffe-Brown, 1880–1955." *Oceania* 26:239–51.

Evans-Pritchard, E. E. 1951. *Social Anthropology.* Glencoe, Ill.: The Free Press.

Fenton, William N. 1962. Introduction to a new edition of *The League of the Iroquois,* by Lewis H. Morgan. New York: Corinth Books.

Firth, Raymond. 1957. *Man and Culture.* New York: The Humanities Press.

Fortes, Meyer. 1956. "Alfred Reginald Radcliffe-Brown, F.B.A., 1881–1955: A Memoir." *MAN* 56:149–53.

Fortes, Meyer, ed. 1949. Preface to *Social Structure: Studies Presented to A. R. Radcliffe-Brown.* Oxford: Oxford University Press.

Fortune, Reo. 1932. "Incest." *Encyclopaedia of the Social Sciences,* vol. 7. New York: Macmillan.

Fraser, James G. 1910. *Totemism and Exogamy,* vol. 1. London: Macmillan.

Freud, Sigmund. 1930. *Civilization and Its Discontents.* New York: Jonathan Cape and Harrison Smith.

Fung, Yu-lan. 1922. "Why China Has No Science." *International Journal of Ethics* 33:3.

Gallatin, Albert. 1845. *Notes on the Semi-Civilized Nations of Mexico,* etc. Transactions of the American Ethnological Society, 1.

Gerard, Ralph W. 1940. "Organism, Society and Science." *Scientific Monthly* 50:403–12.

——. 1942. "Higher Levels of Integration." In *Levels of Integration in Biological and Social Systems,* Robert Redfield, ed. In *Biological Symposia,* vol. 8, Jaques Cattell, ed. Lancaster, Penn.: Jaques Cattell Press.

——. 1949. *Unresting Cells.* New York: Harper.

Goldenweiser, Alexander. 1914. "The Social Organization of the Indians of North America." *Journal of American Folk-Lore* 27:411–36.

——. 1918. "The Diffusion of Clans in North America." *American Anthropologist* 20:118–20.

——. 1940. "Leading Contributions of Anthropology to Social Theory." In *Contemporary Social Theory,* Harry Elmer Barnes and Howard Becker, eds. New York: Appleton-Century.

——. 1941. "Recent Trends in American Anthropology." *American Anthropologist* 43:151–63.

Gumplowicz, Ludwig. 1899. *The Outlines of Sociology.* Trans. F. W. Moore. Philadelphia: American Academy of Political and Social Science.

Hacker, Andrew. 1964. "Introduction: Corporate America." In *The Corporation Take-Over,* Andrew Hacker, ed. New York: Harper and Row.

Haddon, A. C. 1934. *History of Anthropology.* 2d ed. London: The Thinkers Library.

Hall, Edward T. 1968. "Proxemics." *Current Anthropology* 9: nos. 2, 3.

Herrick, C. Judson. 1956. *The Evolution of Human Nature.* Austin: University of Texas Press.

Herring, Pendleton. 1967. *Group Representation before Congress.* New York: Russell and Russell.

Herskovits, Melville J. 1942. "On the Values in Culture." *Scientific Monthly* 54:557–60.

——. 1953. *Franz Boas: The Science of Man in the Making.* New York: Scribner.

Hodgen, Margaret T. 1964. *Early Anthropology in the Sixteenth and Seventeenth Centuries.* Philadelphia: University of Pennsylvania Press.

Honigmann, John J. 1964. "Cultural Determinism." *A Dictionary of the Social Sciences,* Julius Gould and William L. Kolb, eds. Glencoe, Ill.: The Free Press.

Hubbert, M. King. 1950. "Energy from Fossil Fuels." In *Centennial.* Washington, D.C.: American Association for the Advancement of Science.

Huxley, Julian S. 1940. "Science, Natural and Social." *The Scientific Monthly* 50:5–16.

——. 1955. "Evolution, Cultural and Biological." In *Yearbook of Anthropology,* William L. Thomas, Jr., ed. New York: Wenner-Gren Foundation for Anthropological Research.

Jaszi, Oscar. 1934. "Socialism." *Encyclopaedia of the Social Sciences,* vol. 14.

Kluckhohn, Clyde. 1939. "The Place of Theory in Anthropological Studies." *Philosophy of Science* 6:328–34.

——. 1943. "Bronislaw Malinowski, 1884–1942." *Journal of American Folklore* 56:208–19.

——. 1949. *Mirror for Man.* New York: McGraw-Hill.

——. 1951. "A Comparative Study of Values of Five Cultures," a prefatory statement in *Navaho Veterans: A Study of Changing Values,* by Evon Z. Vogt. *Papers of the Peabody Museum of American Archaeology and Ethnology.* Harvard University, vol. 41, no. 1. Cambridge, Mass.

Kroeber, A. L. 1917. "The Superorganic." *American Anthropologist,* n.s., 19:163–213.

——. 1928. "The Anthropological Attitude." *The American Mercury* 13:490–96.

——. 1931. Review of *Growing Up in New Guinea,* by Margaret Mead. *American Anthropologist* 33:248–50.

———. 1935. Review of *Patterns of Culture*, by Ruth Benedict. *American Anthropologist* 37:689–90.

———. 1936. "So-Called Social Science." *Journal of Social Philosophy* 1:317–40.

———. 1939. *Cultural and Natural Areas of North America.* Berkeley: University of California Publications in American Archaeology and Ethnology.

———. 1944. *Configurations of Culture Growth.* Berkeley: University of California Press.

———. 1949. "Values as a Subject of Natural Science Inquiry." *Proceedings of the National Academy of Sciences* 35:261–64.

———. 1952. "The History and Present Orientation of Cultural Anthropology." [1950], first published in *The Nature of Culture*, 1952.

———. 1956. "The Place of Boas in Anthropology." *American Anthropologist* 58: 151–59.

Kroeber, A. L., and Clyde Kluckhohn. 1952. *Culture: A Critical Review of Concepts and Definitions. Papers of the Peabody Museum of American Archaeology and Ethnology.* Harvard University, vol. 47, no. 1. Cambridge, Mass.

LaBarre, Weston. 1954. *The Human Animal.* Chicago: University of Chicago Press.

Lapsley, Arthur Brooks, ed. 1906. *The Writings of Abraham Lincoln*, vol. 7, 1863–1865. New York: Putnam.

Lowie, R. H. 1917a. *Culture and Ethnology.* New York: Boni and Liveright.

———. 1917b. Review of W. H. R. Rivers's articles, "Kin, Kinship," "Marriage: Introduction and Primitive," and "Mother-Right," in *Hastings Encyclopaedia of Religion and Ethics.* In *American Anthropologist* 19:269–72.

———. 1920. *Primitive Society.* New York: Liveright.

———. 1923. Review of *The Andaman Islanders*, by A. R. Brown. *American Anthropologist* 25:575.

———. 1933. "Marriage." *Encyclopaedia of the Social Sciences*, vol. 10.

———. 1934. "Social Organization." *Encyclopaedia of the Social Sciences*, vol. 14.

———. 1936. "Cultural Anthropology: A Science." *American Journal of Sociology* 42:310–20.

——. 1937. *The History of Ethnological Theory.* New York: Farrar and Rinehart.

——. 1940. "American Culture History." *American Anthropologist* 42:409–28.

——. 1946. "Evolution in Cultural Anthropology: A Reply to Leslie White." *American Anthropologist* 48:223–33.

——. 1947. "Franz Boas." National Academy of Science, *Biographical Memoirs,* vol. 24.

Lynd, Robert S. 1939. *Knowledge for What?* Princeton: Princeton University Press.

Malinowski, Bronislaw. 1922. *Argonauts of the Western Pacific.* London: Dutton.

——. 1929. "Social Anthropology." *Encyclopaedia Britannica,* 14th ed.

——. 1930a. "Kinship." *MAN* 30: no. 2.

——. 1930b. Foreword to *The Red Men of Nigeria,* by Captain J. R. Wilson-Haffenden. Philadelphia: Lippincott.

——. 1932. Introduction to *Sorcers of Dubu,* by Reo F. Fortune. New York: Dutton.

——. 1939. "The Group and the Individual in Functional Analysis." *American Journal of Sociology* 44:938–64.

Marx, Karl. 1912. *Capital.* London: William Glaisher.

Mason, O. T. 1895. *Influence of Environment upon Human Industries or Arts.* Smithsonian Institution Annual Report. Washington, D.C.: United States Government Printing Office.

Mead, Margaret. 1968. "Benedict, Ruth." *International Encyclopedia of the Social Sciences.*

Milbrath, Lester W. 1963. *The Washington Lobbyists.* Chicago: Rand McNally.

——. 1968. "Lobbying." *International Encyclopedia of the Social Sciences.*

Millikan, R. A. 1931. In *Living Philosophies.* New York: Simon and Schuster.

Moon, Parker T. 1926. *Imperialism and World Politics.* New York: Macmillan.

Murdock, G. P. 1932. "The Science of Culture." *American Anthropologist* 34:200–215.

Ostwald, W. 1909. *Energetische Grundlagen der Kulturwissenschaft.* Leipzig: W. Klinkhardt.

———. 1916. "The System of the Sciences." Rice Institute Pamphlet 2, no. 3. Houston.

Park, Robert E. and Ernest W. Burgess, eds. 1921. *Introduction to the Science of Sociology.* Chicago: University of Chicago Press.

Parsons, Elsie Clews. 1936. "Early Relations between Hopi and Keres." *American Anthropologist* 38:554–60.

Poincaré, Henri. 1913. Introduction to the "Value of Science." In *The Foundations of Science.* New York: Science Press.

Putnam, Palmer C. 1953. *Energy in the Future.* New York, London, and Toronto: Van Nostrand.

Radcliffe-Brown, A. R. 1931a. "The Present Position of Anthropological Studies." British Association for the Advancement of Science. Reprinted in Introduction to *Method in Social Anthropology,* M. N. Srinivas, ed. Chicago: University of Chicago Press.

———. 1931b. "The Social Organization of Australian Tribes." *Oceania,* 1: no. 4.

———. 1934. "Sanction, Social." *Encyclopaedia of the Social Sciences,* vol. 13.

———. 1941. "The Study of Kinship Systems." *Journal of the Royal Anthropological Institute* 71:1–8. Reprinted in Radcliffe-Brown, *Structure and Function in Primitive Society: Essays and Addresses,* 1952.

———. 1947. "Evolution, Social or Cultural?" *American Anthropologist* 49:78–83.

———. 1957. *A Natural Science of Society.* Glencoe, Ill.: The Free Press.

Raisky, L. G. 1932. *The Struggle Against Opportunism: An Appraisal of Daniel De Leon.* New York: The Socialist Labor Party (The New York Labor News Co.)

Redfield, Robert. 1941. *The Folk Culture of Yucatan.* Chicago: University of Chicago Press.

———. 1955. Introduction to *Social Anthropology of North American Tribes,* Fred Eggan, ed. Enlarged ed. Chicago: University of Chicago Press.

Richards, Audrey. 1957. "The Concept of Culture in Malinowski's Work." In *Man and Culture,* Raymond Firth, ed. London: Routledge.

Rivers, W. H. R. 1922. "The Unity of Anthropology." *Journal of the Royal Anthropological Institute* 52.

Russell, B. n. d. *How to Become a Mathematician.* Girard, Kansas: E. Haldeman-Julius.

Salomon, Gottfried. 1934. "Social Organism." *Encyclopaedia of the Social Sciences,* vol. 14.

Sapir, Edward. 1917. "Do We Need a Superorganic?" *American Anthropologist* 19:441–47.

——. 1927. "Anthropology and Sociology." In *The Social Sciences and Their Interrelations,* Alexander Goldenweiser and William F. Ogburn, eds. Boston: Houghton Mifflin.

——. 1932. "Cultural Anthropology and Psychiatry." *Journal of Abnormal and Social Psychology* 27:229–42.

Seligman, Brenda Z. 1929. "Incest and Descent: Their Influence on Social Orgaization." *Journal of the Royal Anthropological Institute* 59.

——. 1950a. "The Problem of Incest and Exogamy: A Restatement." *American Anthropologist* 52:305–16.

——. 1950b. Letter to Leslie A. White, October 6, 1950.

Shapley, H. 1967. *The View from a Distant Star.* New York: Basic Books.

Sharp, Lauriston. 1968. "Ralph Linton." In *International Encyclopedia of the Social Sciences.*

Singer, Charles. 1956. "Epilogue: East and West in Retrospect." In *A History of Technology,* Charles Singer et al., eds., II, 753–76. New York, London: Oxford University Press.

Smith, Watson and John M. Roberts. 1954. *Zuni Law: A Field of Values. Papers of the Peabody Museum of American Archaeology and Ethnology,* Harvard University, vol. 43, no. 1. Cambridge, Mass.

Soddy, F. 1912. *Matter and Energy.* London: Williams and Norgate.

Sorokin, Pitirim. 1928. *Contemporary Sociological Theories.* New York, London: Harper.

Spencer, Herbert. 1898. *The Principles of Sociology,* vol. 1, pt. 2. New York: Appleton.

Spier, Leslie. 1931. "Historical Interrelation of Culture Traits: Franz Boas' Study of Tsimshian Mythology." In *Methods in*

Social Sciences: A Case Book, Stuart A. Rice, ed. Chicago: University of Chicago Press.

Spiro, Melford E. 1951. "Culture and Personality." *Psychiatry* 14:19–46.

Steigerwalt, A. K. 1964. *The National Association of Manufacturers, 1895–1914, A Study in Business Leadership.* Ann Arbor, Mich.: Bureau of Business Research, Graduate School of Business Administration, University of Michigan.

Steward, Julian H. 1936. "The Economic and Social Basis of Primitive Bands." In *Essays in Honor of A. L. Kroeber*, R. H. Lowie, ed. Berkeley: University of California Press.

——. 1937. "Ecological Aspects of Southwestern Society." *Anthropos* 32:87–104.

Thomson, J. A. n. d. "Darwin's Predecessors." In *Evolution in Modern Thought.* New York: Boni and Liveright.

Turner, Ralph E. 1941. *The Great Cultural Traditions,* 2 vols. New York and London: McGraw-Hill.

Tylor, Sir Edward B. 1871. *Primitive Culture: Researches into the Development of Mythology, Philosophy, Religion, Language, Art, and Custom.* 5th ed., 1913. 2 vols. Reprinted, 1927. London: John Murray.

——. 1889. "On a Method of Investigating the Development of Institutions; applied to Laws of Marriage and Descent." *The Journal of the Anthropological Institute,* vol. 18. London.

Vierkandt, A. 1934. "Georg Simmel (1858–1918)." *Encyclopaedia of the Social Sciences,* vol. 14.

Vogt, Evon Z. 1951. *Navaho Veterans: A Study of Changing Values. Papers of the Peabody Museum of American Archaeology and Ethnology,* Harvard University, vol. 41, no. 1. Cambridge, Mass.

——. 1955. *Modern Homesteaders: The Life of a Twentieth-Century Frontier Community.* Cambridge: Harvard University Press.

Vogt, Evon Z. and John M. Roberts. 1956. "A Study of Values." *Scientific American* 195.

Vogt, Evon Z. an Ethel M. Albert, eds. 1966. *The People of Rimrock: A Study of Values in Five Cultures.* Cambridge: Harvard University Press.

Walker, J. R. 1917. "The Sun Dance and Other Ceremonies of the Oglala Division of the Teton Dakota." *Anthropological Papers of the American Museum of History,* vol. 16, pt. 2.

Washburn, S. L. 1968. "One Hundred Years of Biological Anthropology." In *One Hundred Years of Anthropology.* J. C. Brew, ed. Cambridge: Harvard University Press.

Watson, Frank Dekker. 1922. *The Charity Organization Movement in the United States.* New York: Macmillan. Reprinted in *Poverty, U.S.A.: The Historical Record.* New York: Arno Press and the *New York Times,* 1971.

Webb, Sidney. 1908 [1889]. "Historic." In *The Fabian Essays in Socialism* (1889), G. B. Shaw, ed. Boston: Ball.

Wedgwood, Camilla H. 1929. "Endogamy." *Encyclopaedia Britannica,* 14th ed.

White, A. D. 1896. *History of the Warfare of Science with Theology in Christendom.* New York: Appleton.

White, Leslie A. 1939. "Mind is *Minding.*" *The Scientific Monthly* 48:169–71. Reprinted in White, *The Science of Culture,* 1949 and 1969.

———. 1942. "On the Use of Tools by Primates." *Journal of Comparative Psychology* 34:369–74. Reprinted in *The Science of Culture,* 1949.

———. 1947. "On the Expansion of the Scope of Science." *Journal of the Washington Academy of Sciences* 37:181–210. Reprinted in *The Science of Culture,* 1949.

———. 1948. "The Definition and Prohibition of Incest." *American anthropologist* 50:416–35. Reprinted in *The Science of Culture,* 1949.

———. 1949. *The Science of Culture: A Study of Man and Civilization.* New York: Farrar Straus.

———. 1954. Review of *Culture: A Critical Review of Concepts and Definitions,* by A. L. Kroeber and Clyde Kluckhohn. *American Anthropologist* 56:461–68.

———. 1957. "How Morgan Came to Write 'Systems of Consanguinity and Affinity.' " Papers of the Michigan Academy of Sciences, Arts, and Letters 42:257–68.

———. 1958. "On 'Legalized Incestuous Marriage.' " *MAN* 58:116.

———. 1959a. The Concept of Culture. *American Anthropologist*

61:227–51. Reprinted in the Bobbs-Merrill Reprint Series in the Social Sciences A-238.

——. 1959b. *The Evolution of Culture.* New York: McGraw-Hill.

——. 1960. "Four Stages in the Evolution of Minding." In *Evolution After Darwin.* Vol. 2, *The Evolution of Man,* Sol Tax, ed. Chicago: University of Chicago Press.

——. 1962. "Symboling: A Kind of Behavior." *Journal of Psychology* 53:311–18.

——. 1963. "The Ethnography and Ethnology of Franz Boas." *Texas Memorial Museum Bulletin,* no. 6. Austin, Texas.

——. 1964. Introduction to *Ancient Society,* by Lewis H. Morgan. Camridge: Harvard University Press.

——. 1966. *The Social Organization of Ethnological Theory.* Rice University Studies, vol. 52, no. 4. Houston.

——. 1968. "Nations as Sociocultural Systems." *Ingenor.* Ann Arbor: The University of Michigan College of Engineering.

——. 1969. *The Science of Culture: A Study of Man and Civilization,* 2d. ed. New York: Farrar, Straus and Giroux.

White, Leslie with Beth Dillingham. 1973. *The Concept of Culture.* Minneapolis: Burgess.

Whitehead, Alfred North. 1911. *Introduction to Mathematics.* New York: Holt, Home University Library.

Wiener, Norbert. 1950. *The Human Use of Human Beings.* Boston: Houghton Mifflin.

Wilson, Woodrow. 1913. *The New Freedom: A Call for the Emancipation of the Generous Energies of a People.* New York and Garden City: Doubleday, Page.

Wissler, C. 1917. *The American Indian.* New York: Oxford University Press.